DEATH BY LEGEND

MATT BILLE

HANGAR 1 PUBLISHING

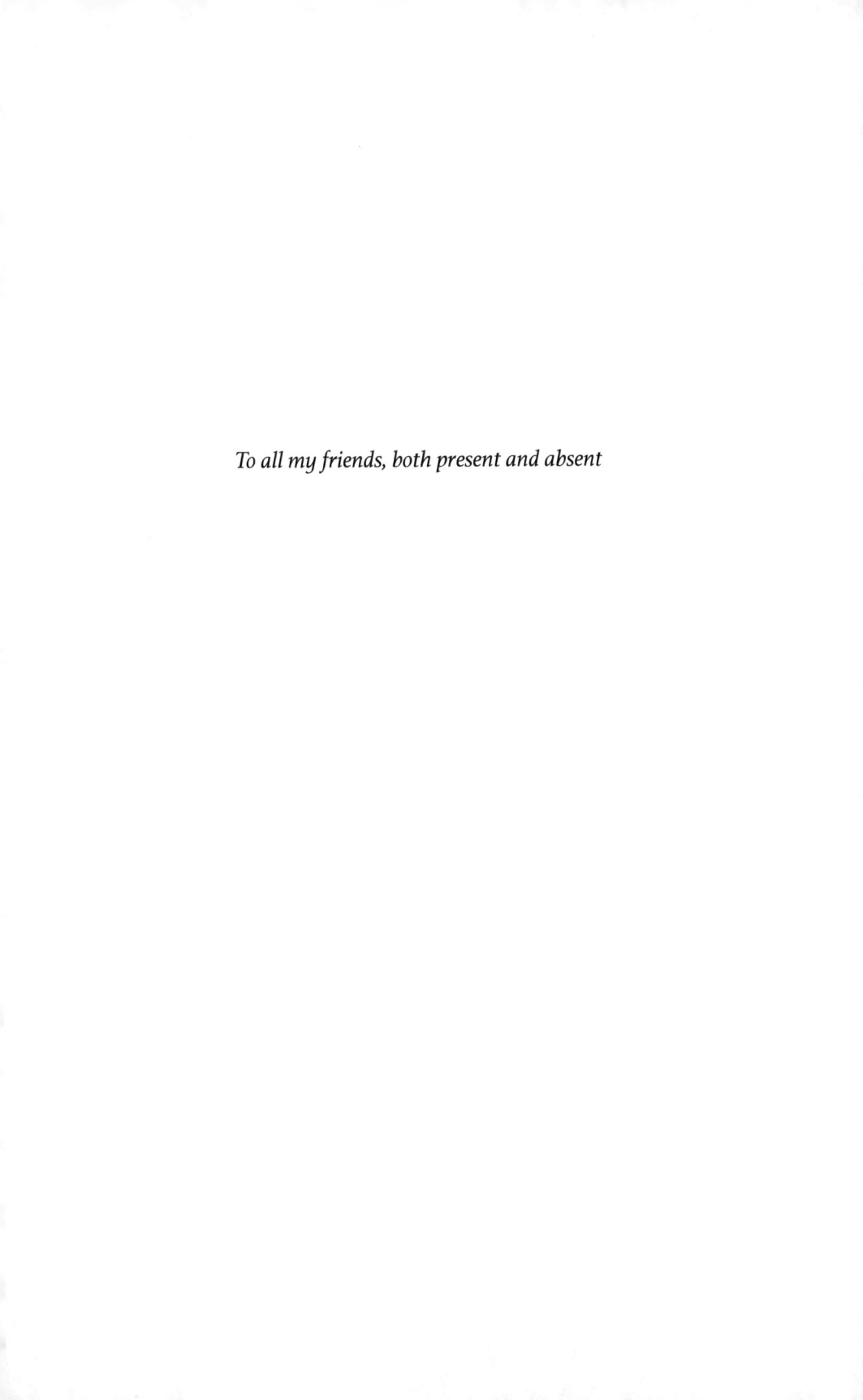

To all my friends, both present and absent

PROLOGUE

G reg Preston thought about dying.

Under the circumstances, it was hard to think of anything else. He stood in a nearly-dark warehouse, a manmade cave of emptiness and shadow. He stared at the only source of light, an open loading door admitting the pallid glow of streetlamps.

He felt the sweat on the palm of his right hand where it clutched the hard, alien shape of a .45 semi-automatic pistol. The gun was unnecessary, really, the police insisted. They hadn't convinced him.

A shifting in the shadows behind him reminded Greg he wasn't the only person there. Five steps back, crouched a heavily armed police officer. On the floor above were fifteen others, and twenty more were hidden in the warehouse office or the vans outside. He wondered for the hundredth time if they would be enough.

It was all a trap for something most people would never believe existed. Not in the twenty-first century, and certainly not in southern California. Greg Preston was the bait, and no matter how many cops backed him up, he still felt naked and vulnerable.

An odd bit of old English poetry swirled into his head. Now, who wrote that? Allingham, maybe.

Up the airy mountain,
Down the rushy glen,
We daren't go a-hunting
For fear of little men.

And if they got him, he'd just be one more in a lengthening series of deaths. What would the coroner even call their fate? Death by legend?

Greg held the gun even tighter.

1

"**W**alt is really dead."

Greg spoke in the barest whisper, audible only to himself. "Walt is really gone."

He turned the phrase over and over in his mind, trying to grasp the impact of it as he looked out the airliner's window at nothing. His friend Walt Revis had died at the age of twenty-nine, four weeks short of his scheduled wedding to Julie Sperling.

Julie had called him and tracked him down on vacation at Paradise Island in the Bahamas. Not just to tell him the tragic news but to mumble almost incoherently that there was something about the death—

The murder, Greg reminded himself. Someone had murdered Walt, and Julie's choking voice had said there was something about the crime she thought he could help with.

What the hell could she mean? He hadn't seen them in almost a year. He hadn't kept in regular contact with Julie beyond the usual social media stuff since they'd graduated together, although he and Walt had emailed or DM'd more often. Julie and Walt had stayed in L.A. while Greg moved to Sacramento, and the romance that never quite worked out between Greg and Julie had worked out very well with Julie and Walt.

"Sorry." The woman in the adjoining seat smiled as she dabbed at the spot of diet cola she'd dripped onto the sleeve of Greg's denim shirt.

"It's okay." Under other circumstances, Greg would have found her dazzling. As it was, she was at least a welcome distraction. The petite blonde in the cranberry suit had the kind of attractiveness Greg always noticed, a mixture of looks and energy not many women possessed. The suit was perfectly tailored to her slim figure, and a ruffled blouse of ivory silk showed beneath the jacket. Given all that, the almost stereotypical California beach smile verged on overkill.

"I suppose I could blame turbulence, but it's easier to tell the truth and admit I'm clumsy." She extended a hand, belying her claim to klutziness by making even that small gesture look graceful. "I'm Karen Montrose."

"The reporter?"

She nodded.

"I remember watching you a few years ago in college. Still with KTSG?"

"Still there. And you are?"

"Greg Preston." He got around to shaking the hand she'd offered. Her grip was strong.

"That sounds familiar. What do you do?"

"I'm a writer."

She snapped her fingers. "*Science or Pseudoscience?* And, no, I didn't read it. I just remember the documentary based on it."

Greg chuckled. "That's okay. They hired someone else to revise my book for the documentary, which ticked me off and still does, but I thought the show came out all right."

"So did I. It sure beats the crap that usually makes the air on subjects like that, not to mention the online cesspools. I'm going to reach through my phone and strangle the next person who calls me with proof the President is an alien lizardman or to tell me they saw sasquatch."

"I don't know yet if we can close the file on sasquatch, but that's for another time," Greg said.

"Interesting. Are you on a book tour now?"

"No. I'm not in the tier of authors who get expense-paid book tours. I make a living, though. In the writing world, that makes me an overnight success."

"In the reporting world, I'm an old lady. If you hit thirty and you're not at least a weekend anchor yet, they start talking about you in the past tense."

"I always thought you were darn sharp. What does one need to do to get an anchor slot?"

"Thank you. Honest answer? You either break some earth-shaking stories, or you kiss the right butts. And you can guess what some managers think 'kissing butts' is still a euphemism for in our enlightened Me-Too century. They don't think I've done enough of either."

"If you don't mind my asking, does local TV really still have clout?"

Karen nodded as if she appreciated the question. "It surprises some people, but yes, it still matters. Local contacts matter, and people talk more to me than bloggers. Professional visuals matter a lot. Plus, we sometimes hold back some juicy details from our internet feed if we've got something exclusive. Trying to stay relevant makes us more personality-driven, so we come full circle to wanting younger and prettier."

"And there's still some double standard there. Women vs. men."

"You bet there is. We brought in an anchor from San Diego named John Delvecchio. He's sixty-two, but he looks like George Clooney's brother, and he's the most popular anchor in the state. But he's not old. He's 'distinguished.'"

Greg was going to reply, but the P.A. system took priority. *"Ladies and gentlemen, we are beginning our descent into Los Angeles International Airport. Please return your tray tables..."*

Karen handed her drink to the attendant, who materialized at the end of their two-seat row. "If you watched me in college, I must have just started. I graduated from LAU eleven years ago and got my start a year later."

"Same school, two years later. By my senior year, you were already famous. Been back to the campus lately?"

"I gathered reactions there to the serial killer case in Inglewood last year. I wanted to see whether the students thought about their city outside their little island. The general response was, 'It wasn't here, so no big deal.' "

"I haven't been back in six years, but it sounds like nothing's changed."

"The living as a writer must be pretty good. Not on a book tour, but you're still flying first class."

Greg tried not to be annoyed—*she's a reporter, prying is like breathing*—as reality pushed back into his mind. "It was the only seat open. Emergency trip." He let out a long breath. "Today started on the twelve-thirty AM flight from Miami through DFW. No nonstops available. Not surprising these days."

"Sorry. Anything I can do?"

"No. You probably already covered it, anyway."

"That's intriguing, but all of a sudden, you don't look like a man to ask questions of, so I won't."

"I appreciate that." He felt the thump as the landing gear went down.

Karen busied herself looking in her purse. "If there's a story you still want to tell sometime, though, give me a call." She turned to hand him her card and saw the anger beginning to knit his brows. "Sorry. I was going to add, feel free to give me a call in any case." She flashed the smile again. "Maybe we can talk about sasquatch."

He nodded. "Apology accepted." He fished a card from his wallet and swapped it for hers.

"Thank you."

As the plane turned onto final approach, Greg turned back to the window and back to his thoughts. *Walt. Why Walt? Who would kill him? And why does Julie think I'm going to be of any use whatsoever?*

2

Ben Slick had worked his usual shift the night before Greg Preston's flight. At least, that's what he started out to do.

Roosevelt Municipal Golf Course was dark and quiet when Ben, almost done with his last circuit of the course's boundaries, stopped his John Deere buggy and clambered out with a flashlight. He'd written up that sagging bit of chain-link fence last night and damned if the stoned kids who passed for greenskeepers these days hadn't ignored it. Hell, it looked worse.

It was true what everyone said: you couldn't get good help anymore. He'd been a greenskeeper on this course all the way through college, but that was forty-five years ago. Now he was getting charity from his son's friend, a Board of Directors member who'd gotten Ben an easy part-time job as "evening greens inspector." All he had to do was patrol the course at the end of the day, clean up a little, and make notes about brown spots on the greens or damaged bushes some frustrated golfer had beaten up with a nine-iron. Ben knew he was lucky and hadn't had anything else to do since Grace died. He also knew the guys who came in at six in the morning to fix his write-ups resented the hell out of the old man who only worked after the heat of the day had long passed.

Ben tried to do a thorough job because he figured he owed that much to everybody involved. He told himself that desire, not plain old loneliness, drove him to make more patrols than he needed to and be the last person to leave the complex every night.

It really was a nice evening. Up here near Griffith Park, the city was muted, the breeze was enough to keep the insects from getting too bad, and—well, it would be good if the daytime help hadn't ignored the damned fence.

Ben inspected the base of the fence, which ran along the shallow cement-lined ditch that carried the runoff from the massive amounts of water and chemicals dumped on the course. It always smelled weird along the ditch, even to a man who'd been around golf courses forever. The head greenskeeper here made his own grass tonic, a crazy mixture that included household ammonia and Listerine and Coors beer, which you'd think would kill anything it touched but actually kept the greens impressively shiny.

The fence was sagging, like someone had been pulling it up from the bottom to get in. That was exactly what Ben suspected, given that the big tree limb that had fallen across the ditch a week before was still there. Someone from the city was supposed to deal with that. Ben didn't know who, and maybe kids had been using it for a bridge. If they'd been on the golf course, though, they hadn't stolen or broken anything as far as he could tell.

He headed back toward the buggy and stopped as he realized he'd seen something else, something that had barely registered at the edge of his vision. He turned to his left and looked along the fence.

Somebody was crouching in the rough on his side of the fence. He could only see the outline, but it was someone, someone trying to be a statue but moving just a little.

Ben opted not to yell or put the flashlight on the furtive shape. Kids in this city could be damned dangerous, and the smart thing to do was walk casually back to the buggy and zoom off before he grabbed the cell phone and called night security.

His heart was thumping in a way he hadn't felt since Vietnam, a way that reminded him bizarrely of a washing machine thrashing with an off-center load. He kept the patch of rough and shadow in the corner of one eye as he walked fifteen deliberate and very long steps to the buggy. He felt the pounding in his chest relax just a bit as he slid into the driver's seat and reached for the key.

The arm that exploded from under the buggy and yanked him out moved so fast he didn't really see it, only felt it, felt the disorienting force and the terrifying grip and the hard slap as he hit the ground. The blow that followed was even faster, and he never saw it at all.

3

It was 10:30 on a hot Tuesday morning in August when the silver Boeing 777 pulled up to Gate 76 in the giant, yellowish concrete edifice that was the main terminal of LAX. Greg stepped off the plane, looking around even though he knew Julie couldn't be waiting at the gate. With a quick nod and a choppy wave in Karen's direction, he took a death grip on his laptop case and sports duffel and submerged himself in the streams of people.

He'd never liked LAX. It was an impersonal place, with blank cream-colored walls and blank-faced workers to match. The attempts to freshen up the terminal with atriums and plants hadn't helped. The plants always looked like they were just about to turn brown and die. And what always struck him on arriving in L.A. was the dirty, stifling, too-warm air. It could be smelled, even tasted, but could never be precisely described. He only knew he hated it.

He paused a moment to fish out his cell phone and activate it. No new messages. He pocketed it and hurried on.

Greg emerged into the utilitarian lobby housing his flight's baggage claim and immediately began looking for Julie, but there was no need. The moment he stepped out of the people-flow, Julie wrapped him in an embrace that was almost a tackle. He dropped his bag and returned the hug, holding her close enough to feel her heartbeat, and neither spoke for a minute.

"God, I'm glad you're here," she finally said.

Greg's first question slipped out of his mouth before his brain could grab hold and strangle it. "Do they know who killed Walt yet?"

She shook her head, sending her long black hair dancing. Greg noticed that even looking drawn and tired, she still stopped the male traffic around her. It was her eyes, he mused, even more than her naturally athletic figure or overall pretty-girl-next-door looks. Those deep emerald eyes had caught his attention the moment he'd met her, and they weren't any less arresting even now, despite the redness and puffiness lining them. Julie wasn't wearing her trademark gold-leaf earrings. He'd hardly ever seen her without them. Her lightweight tan suit looked expensive but needed pressing. Still, she could have been forgiven for being a lot less organized than she was.

"I'm so glad you came," she said. "I need you."

"Well, here I am," he said, trying for a reassuring tone.

They embraced again, and he saw a tear escape one eye. She dabbed at it with her finger and pulled back a little. "Sorry."

"Don't be. For God's sake, you're entitled. What do we do now?"

"Come with me."

* * *

They stepped outside into the smog-diffused yet still oppressive sunshine. Greg's shirt and khakis almost instantly wilted against his body. Crossing a broad street that looked like a racetrack for shuttle buses, they entered the parking structure, where Julie led him to an aggressive-looking black sports car.

Greg nodded appreciatively at the nearly-new Ford Mustang fastback. "Heck of a nice car," he said. "Is that an actual manual transmission?"

She managed a little smile. "Driving them since I was fifteen. And they're a big advantage these days. Not many people can steal it."

Julie couldn't hide the forced edge of her humor, but he had to admire her effort.

She opened the hatch, and he dumped his bags inside. "I'll drive," she said. "I'll bet you still can't find your way around L.A. any more than the day you got here from Pincushion, Arizona."

Greg smiled at their old joke. "Pinecotton wasn't big enough to have pincushions. We just stuck pins in each other. Helped relieve the boredom."

"When's the last time you were back there?" she asked.

"Never."

"Seriously? Not since graduation?"

Greg shrugged. "There didn't seem to be a reason. I never liked the place—you know that. L.A. was like Mars when I got here, but this got to be more home than Arizona. Remember, my folks are in Scottsdale now. They didn't want to move there, but they turned sixty, and it's state law."

"Huh?"

"Sorry. Arizona joke. But really, I don't know if old Pincushion is even still there."

"You look good. Tennis must still agree with you."

"I saw your comments on the pic I posted from the Sacramento Amateur Open," he said. "I was pretty happy with making the quarterfinals."

"I read all your posts. I've been promising for two years I'd take tennis up again, but—" the thought seemed to run out, and she pressed her lips tightly together. "Let's get going."

Greg closed the hatch for her. He climbed in on the passenger's side, folding his lean six-one frame into the comfortable fighter cockpit seat. Minutes later, after picking their way through the maze of airport traffic, they were on the San Diego Freeway.

The silence in the car was oppressive, a heavy presence that impeded breathing. It was as if Julie had used up her capacity for small talk at the airport, and it wasn't yet time for big talk. Julie didn't turn on the CD player for her usual diet of jazz, and he wasn't about to take the initiative. So he endured the silence as Julie stared holes in the roadway ahead.

It wasn't long before they were cruising north on the Harbor Freeway past their old stomping grounds at Los Angeles University. Julie followed the Harbor to the 8th Street exit, then worked her way north and west until she turned off Wilshire Boulevard into the drive of a twelve-story gray and white apartment building whose pretentiously modest sign labeled it The Westbrook.

The neighborhood was a mix of office buildings and apartments, some new and some old. The Westbrook looked fairly new and very well landscaped and maintained. The parking garage was under the first floor, and Julie pulled the Mustang into a slot numbered 704.

As they collected the baggage and walked inside, Greg scanned the building's security. The elevator from the parking garage ran to only one destination. This was a small, well-lit lobby staffed by a blue-shirted armed guard—a young, fit man, not the retired-or-should-be types so often found in jobs like that. The guard gave Julie a nod of recognition and buzzed open the handsome oak doors behind the security desk. As they passed in, Greg noted the bank of video screens allowing the guard to monitor the garage, several interior areas, and what looked like a service entrance.

Through the doors lay a more decorated inner lobby. Julie pressed a magnetic card into a slot to call the elevator.

"This seems like a safe place," Greg said.

Julie grimaced. "That's what they say. A security building, they call it. Walt thought so, too."

Neither said anything more as they rode to the seventh floor. Greg followed her to 704, which turned out to be a fairly spacious two-bedroom furnished in earth tones and an attractive mix of light and dark wood.

"I like it," he said as Julie closed and double-locked the door behind them.

"So did Walt," she said. Her voice was steady but inescapably tinged with emotion. "We were going to live here. The movers were coming next week." She gestured reluctantly toward cardboard boxes piled against one wall. They were labeled *Walt Stuff*.

"Is your mother still here?"

She shook her head. "Mom and my stepdad went back to Chicago yesterday morning. You won't believe how I had to argue with Mom about me staying here."

"I believe it. I've met your mother, remember?"

"Right. I'm on leave of absence from the law firm, so I could have gone. But damn it, there is no way I am leaving this town until I know what happened to Walt and someone is in jail. Or dead, preferably."

"How about your sister?"

"She couldn't come. I talked to her, but her squadron's on a carrier in the Indian Ocean, watching the Sri Lanka crisis."

"And Walt's folks?"

"They're surviving. His mother was on meds. We had the funeral out in Cypress in the church Walt grew up in. The church we were going to be married in." She bit her lip. "His sisters were both there, but it was weird. They kept glaring at me like it was my fault somehow."

He sighed. "You know it's not. But I hate to think of you dealing with all this alone."

"I'm not exactly helpless."

"I never said that."

"I know. I go back and forth between wanting to kill someone and wanting to cry for a few more days. Can I get you a drink?"

"No, thanks. I want to hear the story."

Julie nodded, and they sank onto a sofa.

Her eyes closed for a moment. "He lived on the fifth floor," she said. "Five-twelve. He moved in just a few months ago when we got engaged. Things were great, Greg."

"I remember when he got the job with *L.A. Life* magazine," Greg said. "That was April last year."

"He loved that job. After those years with the paper, he was getting really big as a feature writer. You know how few people can make a decent living from work like that nowadays?"

"Yes, I do. You have to become a brand, essentially, and then keep it going twenty-four-seven. When I went on this vacation, I paid a teenage genius to keep my social media going to make sure I wasn't forgotten about."

"Walt loved all the work that went into that. That's why he got his *Local Explorations* segment on the PBS show and the Web channel. He loved people and culture the way you did science. The magazine was going to make him assistant editor, did you know that?"

"No, he never mentioned it."

"Probably going to surprise you with it when you came for the wedding."

"Well, we both were determined to be writers someday," Greg said. "We both made it."

"I don't know why I'm taking so long to get to the point," she said. Her hands clutched her knees, viciously wrinkling the material of her pants. "It was only ten days ago. I was working late. I got home about ten and went to Walt's apartment. It was locked, but I heard a noise like someone moving inside. He didn't come when I knocked, and the security bolt was still on when I tried my key. Then I came up here and tried to call him. When he didn't answer, I called the guard." Tears were beginning to squeeze from her eyes. "When he couldn't get an answer, he and the manager broke in—and Walt was already dead."

She buried her face in her hands, and he put an arm around her. Julie leaned back into the embrace.

"The police wouldn't even let me in at first," she said. "God, I had to wait for hours. Then, they brought him out on a stretcher. I had to identify him." She turned her face to his, and he couldn't miss the pain in her eyes. "He was lying on the floor. Someone stabbed him in the back. Some bastard..."

Her voice trailed off into sobs, and she shook her head as if apologizing for her inability to continue. Greg put his other arm around her, and she buried her face in his chest and cried.

He said something useless that was immediately forgotten. When had they last been in this position? he wondered. Just after graduation, when her father died.

Julie drew back a little, fumbling for a box of tissues on the end table. She found them, blew her nose, and wiped her eyes.

"I can't tell it very well," she said. "I've got nothing useful to say anyway. Let me get something to show you instead."

She rose, using a hand on his shoulder to push herself up, and walked a little unsteadily into the room she used as an office. She returned with a manila folio held shut by an elastic cord.

"Here," she said. "This is everything that was in the papers and the local news sites. I put this together right after I called you, with some help from one of the legal secretaries. I'm sure you looked it up when I called, but there's more."

"You're not trying to play cop, are you?"

"No, but if I can help just a little or even convince myself I'm helping..." She shook her head. "Excuse me a minute, okay? I need some tea."

Greg watched her walk into the kitchen. Julie's reaction to any crisis had always involved tea. He supposed it was always good to have something familiar.

He shook his head and opened the folio. So far, all he knew was that Walt had been stabbed. There had to be more if this was so mysterious.

* * *

Julie returned twenty minutes later. She had washed her face, put a silver clasp in her hair to tie it back, and was sipping what Greg guessed was her second cup of tea. He sniffed. Cinnamon apple, just like always.

She sat next to him and offered a cookie. "Remember Huckleberry chocolate chips?"

"Oh, man. One of the two basic food groups along with Tommy burgers." He took a big bite, wondering, as always, how it was possible to bake bliss into a cookie.

Julie smiled at his reaction, but her expression tightened as her gaze was drawn involuntarily to the articles he'd spread on the coffee table.

He turned back to the articles. Most were from the *L.A. Times*. There were also some original internet news pieces and some Web versions of stories from the TV stations. One was by Karen Montrose. It was, not surprisingly, brief and not very informative. As Karen had pointed out, televised stories relied on the visuals and the personalities.

Greg looked at the longest one and picked it up. "If you're sure it's okay, then let me ask you something. This *Times* piece— 'An Unsolved Murder on Wilshire.' Have you read this one?"

"Yes. It's really pretty accurate."

"It's hard to see how it could be." Greg glanced at the clipping again. "Walt was face down, stabbed with his own steak knife. Okay so far.

"An unnamed police source stated no fingerprints were found on the knife," Greg quoted. "Again, not too strange. Anyone can wear gloves."

He glanced at Julie. She nodded, and he went on. "'The same source claimed all the locks, including the security latch, were secure.' Boy, if this were fiction, I'd toss it right now. A locked-room murder is a cliché that's been so overdone even the streaming shows don't use it anymore. You heard someone inside about ten, right?"

"Yes. No doubt at all. Just like footsteps, kind of quick and quiet."

"'A sound like someone trying not to make a sound.'"

"Yes, exactly."

"I stole that from John Irving," he said. "Keep going."

"A police detective named Welles told me some things that aren't in the article. The door lock, the deadbolt, and the latch were all closed. We have cards for the doorknob locks and physical keys for the deadbolts. Walt had his on a ring in the kitchen. I had a copy, and the guard and the super had extras. That's it."

"I'm sure the cops are checking whether there are any others—

whether a prior tenant might have kept a copy, for example. But that couldn't explain the latch."

"That's what the detective said, too. And the fire escape is at the end of the hall. No one could reach his apartment from it on the outside."

"Do the windows open?"

"They do, but there's no balcony."

Greg nodded. He went to the nearest window and raised it, leaning out the few inches he could against the plastic bug screen.

He turned back to Julie. "Did this Welles tell you anything about the windows? Open? Closed?"

"Closed. The screens, too."

"There must be another way. Is his apartment like this one?"

"Exactly like it."

Greg looked around the room. There were air-conditioning vents, but they were barely larger than a familiar #10 envelope.

He closed his eyes and visualized the apartment as a 3D line drawing, a common trick he used when thinking about a problem. He spent a minute filling in the important details and then thinking about what he saw and didn't see.

He opened his eyes and gestured to one of the vents. "Julie, is there an outflow vent bigger than these?"

She nodded. "I don't know if it goes in or out, but there is one big one. In the office."

They stepped out of the bedroom. The office, presumably intended as a second, smaller bedroom, adjoined it. Greg was surprised to see a deadbolt lock on the door.

"Why have a lock on a door *inside* your apartment?" he asked.

"I bring case files home. There's a lot of confidential stuff on my computer, too. I know it's a pretty flimsy door, but being able to lock it makes me feel better."

She unlocked the door and led him in. Maneuvering around the desk, two chairs, and two filing cabinets, she pointed at the louvered grating in the ceiling.

Greg studied it. About two feet wide and eighteen inches tall, it would admit a person. "Did Welles say anything about this?"

She nodded. "He said they checked the duct it goes into. It makes a turn right at the wall—his apartment's on the corner. It's way too small for anyone except a little kid. And the other way, there's a fan."

"Let's take a look anyway. You can see where there used to be two screws holding it, but I guess they fell out." Greg pulled a chair under the grating and climbed up on it. He worked his fingers into the grating and pulled. It came out with a momentary metal-on-metal groan. He set the grating down and looked up at the opening.

Julie stepped out of the room for a moment. She returned with a flashlight and handed it over.

Greg peered into the duct. The conduit itself was large enough—maybe—for a skinny person to wriggle through, but there was indeed a currently stationary fan to his left and a bend to his right.

He pulled his head back down and shoved the grating back into place. "I suppose a homicidal kid is possible," Greg said. "Anything in L.A., right? But he'd have to find a place to get into the duct to begin with, and I don't see how he'd get back up in here carrying the grating with him without leaving a chair or something underneath. This is an eight-foot ceiling."

"I don't know, either." She shuddered. "I can't imagine a kid who'd go to all this trouble to kill someone who..." her voice trailed off.

"Remember that scrawny neighborhood kid they arrested on campus once? He held a student up at knifepoint. He was eleven." Greg paused. "Hope I'm not asking too many questions. I'm sure the cops went over this enough times to make you sick."

She gave another nod that he took to mean she was still okay. They pulled out of the office and closed the door, wandering back into Julie's bedroom.

"Julie, is this why you thought I could be useful? Because the cops can't figure this out?"

She sat on the bed, one hand twisting the ends of her hair. "You were the only person I could think of. Not just because I needed someone I could trust. But I thought I needed help from someone with—well, kind of a creative brain like yours. I never saw anyone take so many courses in so many different things. Your mind just works differently. And maybe I wanted someone who knew as much as you do about weird things that don't make sense."

Greg sat next to her. "I don't know what you mean by weird. You know, I've poked around into unexplained phenomena, but I don't see any reason to think there's anything like that here if that's what you're thinking."

"I never said I thought that. But you have imagination, and when Walt was killed in an apartment locked from the inside, with no prints and no nothing—well, if you won't help me, then screw you! I'm sorry I interrupted your fucking vacation!"

Greg realized he had never heard her use that word.

"Julie, I'm sorry. I didn't say I wouldn't help. I'm just not sure what to do."

"Walt was your friend! Don't you even want to know how he died?"

"Of course I do. And don't think I don't care about you, either. Just because I never proposed didn't mean I didn't care. I'll always care, Julie. Hell, I don't know how this sounds, but I probably stopped being in touch because I cared more than I should."

The words sounded clichéd and unconvincing to Greg, even though he meant them. Julie seemed to understand the sincerity.

"You know, for a while there, if you'd proposed, I would have said yes."

"A psychiatrist might say that's why I didn't ask. I know, I'm all contradictions and no sense emotionally. I always was." He shook his head. "I'm still trying to grasp that Walt's gone. Hell, for our last three years of school, we practically breathed the same air."

"Including sometimes when we didn't want him around. The Three Musketeers—God, that's so corny. I wonder how many million people have called themselves that."

"Lots," Greg said. "Did you ever tell Walt we were each other's 'firsts'?" He instantly wanted to bite the question back, but Julie answered.

"It never came up. You know Walt. He'd never ask anything like that."

There was an awkwardly quiet moment as their eyes met.

"I'm sorry. I had no reason to ask that either. This is about Walt and you." When Julie didn't answer, he went on. "Well, if I'm going to play amateur detective, I suppose I need to visit the crime scene."

"It's sealed off, but I can call Alan."

"Alan?"

"Detective Welles." She made a defensive gesture with her hand. "I met him when I spent those years in the DA's office before Washburn, Cooley, and Marquez made me an offer that would get me away from dealing with wackos in the middle of the night. Anyway, he's in what they call the Homicide Special Section in Robbery-Homicide. They work normal day hours plus being on call, so he should be in. I'm sure he'll help."

"Maybe. And maybe he'll just tell me to butt the hell out. We'll see."

4

D etective Alan Welles met them an hour later in front of 512. They stopped at the white wooden door, which showed no sign of having been forced. It would have looked perfectly normal if not for the yellow "Police Line" tape stretched across it.

Julie introduced the two men. Welles was a husky, prematurely graying man in his early forties. He had a slightly bent nose and brown eyes that constantly shifted their focus. Greg caught the slightest whiff of tobacco residue, and he guessed Welles was a smoker who had just quit or was still trying to. The cop wore a worn gray sports coat that contrasted with a crisp white shirt and a new, classy-looking blue silk tie.

"You're a writer too, she tells me," Welles said. "Whatda you write?"

"Nonfiction science books, plus a couple of novels so far. There was a TV documentary last year based on a book I wrote explaining what qualified as science and what didn't. I wrote it after the pandemic. Maybe you saw it."

Welles shook his head. "Afraid not. I know Julie thinks you can help with this. I'm letting you in partly as a favor to her and partly because, if you were his best friend, maybe something here would look funny to you, and you might actually be useful. First, I need your promise you won't talk—or write—about anything you see in here."

"I'm not here to write a book. And I do appreciate this."

Welles nodded briefly, almost curtly. "This case went to Homicide Special 'cause no one in Rampart Division wanted to try figuring it out. We still haven't done it, either." He detached the tape and unlocked the door.

Greg noticed the smell first. It was a hard-to-describe mixture of the metallic smell/taste of blood and something else that may have been psychological but was still nauseating. He gritted his teeth and followed the detective in. He heard Julie's footsteps behind his own.

The apartment was nothing unusual. It had the same off-white walls as Julie's place, but the cabinets, appliances, and other accents were done in subdued greens and blues instead of earth tones. The door opened into the kitchen, and Welles had halted one step in.

"That's where he was," Welles said, pointing at the green-on-white patterned vinyl of the kitchen floor. Dark traces still showed in the cracks between the simulated tiles. Greg's gaze skipped around the room, noting the remnants of fingerprint powder in several places —charcoal-gray on some surfaces, silvery on others.

"He didn't move much," Welles added. "He was stabbed in the back over here, near the fridge. That cabinet was open, so I guess he was bent down to get something." Welles' index finger flicked out as he talked, jabbing at each location. "He crawled there, just a few feet, trying to get away and maybe going for the landline phone on the wall. But he was stabbed through the lung—sorry, Julie, no nice way to tell it—stabbed so hard there was a bruise on his back from the hilt. It got one of his arteries, too. If it's any consolation, he went quick."

Greg glanced at Julie, who was holding back and keeping one hand braced on the wall. Greg stepped back enough to reach for her hand and squeeze it.

She squeezed back. "It's okay. Go on."

"He was surprised, then," Greg said to Welles.

"Yeah. No struggle."

"And no fingerprints you couldn't account for?"

"Not a damn one. I mean, there are always a few prints you can't ID. But we did a lot of searches, and nothing's left but a couple of old partials."

"All the windows were closed?"

"They were. Even if they weren't, it's a thirty-foot drop to the second-floor balcony. But they were. But that chain lock being on—that's the damnedest thing."

"Did you look at that vent in the office ceiling?"

Welles glared briefly. "Yes, Genius. It goes in and takes a bend. The skinniest guy in town couldn't get in that way."

"What about a kid?"

Welles hesitated a moment. "Nobody bigger than an eight-year-old could do it. The knife was driven in by a man, a pretty strong one. Not many weightlifting midget hit men in the files." One corner of Welles' mouth turned up in what might have been his version of a grin.

"So what are you thinking of? Anything?"

He shrugged. "You got me, Genius. Somebody's more clever than we are. So far. That's the other damn thing. No enemies we know of. No motives."

"He was a magazine writer. Maybe he wrote something somebody didn't like."

Welles shook his head. "For a best friend, you're not keeping in touch very well, are you? He wasn't any kind of crusader. He wrote fluff about local characters and art shows and stuff like that. Who'd kill him for that? And why am I wasting time with you if those are the best questions you got?"

"You're a nice guy?"

"Uh-huh. Anything else you want to see?"

"Let me just walk through the place. I won't touch anything."

Welles shrugged.

Greg glanced first at the bedroom. Nothing of interest. Like Julie,

Walt had converted his apartment's second bedroom to an office, and Greg looked through that room more carefully. An obsolete Macintosh desktop computer, a printer, two external drives, and a modem perched on a fake wood desk. Two tan metal file cabinets and two chairs, one swivel rocker, and one basic wooden straight-back type. An 11x17 framed photograph of Julie on the wall, hanging next to Walt's diploma in a display that didn't balance at all.

"Wow, that's old," he said, gesturing at the Mac.

"It's his hobby computer," Julie said. "The police have his tablet."

He noticed Julie following closely now, though she still looked unsettled. "Have you been through his things here?"

She nodded. "Alan brought me through to see if there was anything missing. Nothing was that I noticed."

"It doesn't look like anything was touched," Welles said from behind them. "The killer just wanted him."

"It's too neat," Greg said, rubbing the back of his neck. "One thing I do know about Walt is that his desk was always a mess."

"I taught him to be more organized," Julie said. "It was rough going for a while, but eventually, he decided he liked it."

Greg nodded. She'd worked on him the same way.

There was a transparent plastic file box on the desk, but Greg didn't see anything relevant in it. The top drawer of the nearest file cabinet was open an inch, and Greg gestured at it. "May I look in here?"

"We dusted it already. Go ahead."

"That drawer was for articles in progress," Julie said, something Greg had already noted from the neatly handwritten label on the front. Julie's handwriting.

"I don't know if it was found open like that or not," Julie said.

"I don't remember, either," Welles said. The Rampart guy missed it in the photos. We ain't perfect."

Greg pulled the drawer open and riffled through the manila folders. All had suitably innocuous labels like "Russian Exhibit" and "Aquarium."

"What was the last thing he was working on?"

"A story on a museum," Welles said. "We checked it out, but we didn't find anything."

"That's the file on the desk," Julie said. "The police looked at it."

"'Anglo Museum?' "

"Right. The Museum of Anglo-American Culture."

"There's a museum for Anglo-American culture? Must be controversial as hell."

"You have no idea."

Greg opened the file. "Not much here. Clippings, brochure, Google Earth printouts...usual press releases." He pulled out the largest item in the file, a map of the museum area, and spread it on the desk. It was a large-scale plat, apparently something Walt had gotten from City Planning. In Walt's squarish hand-printing were notes about what he'd observed on a visit. Nothing stuck out as critical, though. No one would kill Walt over annotations like "drainage canal," "rear fence," and "stand of old trees."

"He hadn't even started writing it yet, but he was really into it," Julie said. "He spent a lot of time out there already. He had the idea that the concept, politics, and controversies might be a good book topic."

"He should have some other notes, then."

"We got 'em, Genius,' Wells said. "Like I told you, nothing panned out. You'll get 'em back, Counselor."

"I thought I read some news items about that museum," Greg said. "The controversy got pretty serious, didn't it?"

"Sure, but it's not the kind people get killed over," Welles replied. "There's a protest group, but they check out clean. Look, I'm going to have to kick you two out of here. I got work to do."

"We understand," Julie said. "Thanks so much for coming out."

Welles gave her a nod and that momentary half-smile again. "Anything for you, Counselor. I'm on the response squad this week, so I want to finish my day and maybe get a nap before somebody beeps me. Either of you come up with anything that might help, give me a call. Right?"

"Promise," Greg said.

Julie was out the door first and seemed visibly relieved to be in the hall again. Welles relocked the door, gave them a casual wave, and headed at a brisk pace for the elevator.

"He's a good man," Julie said. "I'm really glad he was around."

"He seems dedicated enough," Greg said. "Acts really casual, but there's kind of an edge to him. I feel like I'd hate to cross him if I was a bad guy. Do you think he means it when he said they don't see any connection with that museum?"

"Not for a minute," Julie said. "When you work in the DA's office, you learn how to read cops. I think he's interested as hell in that place. He's just not about to tell some amateur, namely you, what theories he's working on. You might talk and screw things up or even get in his way."

"I might, I suppose. But I do want to see that museum. What are its hours?"

* * *

The Museum of Anglo-American Culture was near the south end of Griffith Park. Greg and Julie drove north on the Golden State Freeway, creeping through the heavy traffic of late afternoon as they passed Elysian Park and Dodger Stadium. The dodging and weaving cars reminded Greg of cattle being driven in an old Western film, only shown in slow motion. The area looked like he remembered, but for two things – more high-rises and, again, more homeless people. He mused on the connection.

"I'm amazed you're still awake," Julie said. "I thought the flight and everything else would have you worn out."

"I took a cafergot about an hour before landing," Greg said. "I was starting to feel that old familiar migraine warning. The smog and the travel always give me one unless I stay on top of the symptoms. Anyway, the stuff keeps you alert."

"Still have that problem, huh?"

Greg shrugged. "As Reverend Domeika at the University Chapel used to tell us, we all have our little crosses to bear."

"He's still there, by the way. But I thought there were lots of drugs for migraines."

"I'm allergic to triptan drugs. Big Pharma pulled cafergot because there was no money in it, so my neuro has to get it from India. Now he wants to try Botox injections."

"Botox at thirty," Julie said, chuckling. "You really are a Californian now."

"I didn't say 'yes,'" he replied. "Not yet, anyway."

Julie glanced at the road ahead. "We should see the exit for Los Feliz sometime today."

"Take me through the controversy."

"Well, first of all, it was the idea. It was all conceived and financed by a philanthropist named Tom Windsor. He's about a five-thousandth cousin to the British royal Windsors. I won't try to describe him because you wouldn't believe me."

"Why not?"

"He looks like a character from public television. You'll understand if you meet him. Anyway, he bought what I think was the only undeveloped privately owned piece of land this size left within the city limits. My firm did the legal work: I don't do real estate law, but we all had a piece of this mess. That's how Walt got interested in it, really." There was a moment's hitch in her voice, and then she went on. "Anyway, it was undeveloped because the owner wanted a price no one was insane enough to pay."

"But Windsor paid it."

"He didn't even blink. He's about eighty, and I've heard he wants to blow all his money before his greedy relatives get there hands on it. Anyway, he built his museum on it. He complained that everyone was forgetting the British roots of American culture, and he wanted to showcase them."

"I'm getting the picture," he said, "Racist, colonialist, what else?"

"Lots." She stabbed the horn as a pickup truck cut sharply in front of her. "The only good thing about being an associate is that they work you so late you miss rush hour," she grumbled.

"You handle it better than I do," Greg assured her.

"The hell I do. I just missed the damn exit."

Julie gunned the engine and, in a series of sharp, nerve-grating maneuvers and shifts, forced the Mustang into the right lane. Then she turned back to Greg, her face the picture of composure.

"Pardon the inconvenience, sir," she said in a mock British accent. "We shall have a short delay in arriving at our destination."

Greg chuckled. "Well, since we have time, I'll ask again. How controversial?"

"Enough for death threats against Windsor, which he ignores. A museum devoted entirely to WASPs offends a lot of people, from BLM to the Asian Pacific Citizens League. There's a coalition called MAP—Museums for All People. This is media-land, so you have to have an acronym."

"You seem pretty up on this."

Julie swung the Mustang onto the next exit ramp and began making her way south on the surface streets. "We got Windsor his permits," she said. "That was hell. You should have seen the zoning board hearings. In the end, he spread enough money around to get it done. Some of our people didn't want to work on it, but you know my family were farmers until my dad. I was raised to believe you can do what you want with your own property, and that's what the law says, too."

"Who's behind this MAP?"

"You'll probably see him in a minute."

She turned north, taking successively smaller streets until they were on a winding two-lane road between small hills studded with old trees and large houses.

"There's more to this thing than the MAP people, though," she said. "It turns out Mr. Windsor owns a lot of land in England, near Kent. Do you know what a dolmen is?"

"A megalithic tomb. Usually, there are slabs buried edgewise to hold up a roof slab for the burial chamber. Then it's covered with earth."

"Right. Well, there was one on Windsor's land in England. It's here now."

"He moved a *dolmen*?"

She nodded. "It's not clear just how. I'll tell you more when we see it."

5

The Mustang climbed smoothly and powerfully up the road for a few hundred yards through a landscape dominated by the looming green bulk of Mount Hollywood ahead of them. Greg knew the Hollywood sign was somewhere to his left, but he couldn't see it from this angle. He'd been so engrossed in talking to Julie that he hadn't looked for it on the drive north.

The houses had stopped now, and only trees lined their way. "Like I said, this was the only piece of land like it in the city," she said. "It used to be part of a medium-sized estate bordering Griffith Park, including some small hills and a wooded chunk that borders the city golf course. The original owner died, and the heir put it on the market. Anyway, it's Windsor's estate now."

"It has a pretty rural feel to it," Greg said. "If it wasn't for the smog, you might forget you're in the city at all."

"Well, there's the sign." Julie pointed to a green metal sign announcing the museum was just up ahead. At least, that's what Greg assumed it said—it was hard to tell with black spray paint all over it.

A hundred yards farther on, they came to a brownish fieldstone wall pierced by a wide gate. To one side sat a black and white LAPD cruiser.

The gate was flanked on one side by a solid pillar and on the other by a stone gatehouse. About ten protesters were milled in front of the gate, reminding Greg of a very small colony of disturbed ants. They waved signs at the approaching car and chanted something he couldn't make out.

"This being private property, and it being Windsor's home as well as the museum, lets him use the law to keep the protesters outside," Julie said. "So he has private security all the time, plus the real cops like that guy doing spot checks. So far, no violence—none we know of, anyway. Just threats." Her lips pressed tightly together for a moment. "The Black man in the red shirt is their leader, Robert Martin. He's basically a full-time activist with a pretty good following. He knows how to work the media."

As the gate and protesters vanished around a bend, a two-story Tudor-style mansion came into view. "This is the main museum," she explained. "The dolmen's around the back."

They pulled into a small and almost empty parking lot. Leaving the car, she led him down a flagstone path that dipped between the house and a low hill to their right. Another sign, a bronze plaque set on a column of stones, proclaimed the name and founding date of the museum.

"No one else around," Greg said.

"Rob Martin's gotten a lot of publicity for his protest. This is L.A. No one—not even the people who really are racists—want to go against what's trendy, and Rob Martin is trendy."

They turned the rear corner of the house, and Greg stopped.

Talk about stepping into another world.

Behind the house on the three open sides were long, low banks covered with trees and bushes. They screened out the surrounding landscape, leaving only the thoroughly English presence of the manor.

And the dolmen.

It rose directly in front of them, twice Greg's height and maybe fifty feet across. In a few places, the edges of gray stone slabs showed through the grass and earth of the sides, making the whole look like some great armored monster, curled in slumber yet inescapably menacing.

The sky was overcast now, the dimming light adding to the impression this place had nothing to do with twenty-first-century California. There were smaller displays between the mansion and the tomb, but he gave them no thought. The dolmen dominated the scene so utterly that nothing else mattered.

"Impressive, isn't it?"

Greg shook off the spell at the sound of Julie's voice.

"He brought this from England?" Greg asked in an awed whisper.

"Every grain of dirt," she said, her tone also unconsciously hushed. "That was one part of the controversy. A few years ago, he had the whole thing dug up, packed in crates, and sent to New York. Walt thinks—thought— that he had it shipped labeled as dirt for agricultural experiments or something. It sat in a warehouse on Long Island until last year. Then he brought it down here and recreated it. It's not the original grass, of course, but everything else is at least two thousand years old."

"He sure did a great job with the setting," Greg said. "They could shoot a terrific movie here."

"Anyway, the British government is suing Windsor for violating the Antiquities Act by shipping it over here," Julie went on. "But he's not about to go quietly. He insists he's done a great service for our culture, and he's hired about three law firms, including ours. Maybe he figures if he strings it out forever, the British will give up."

"Will they?"

"Not a chance."

Greg walked around the dolmen, shaking his head. The eccentricity of the Brits was apparently no cliché in this case. Just the concept of moving the dolmen was staggering. Add to that the expense and expertise needed for this restoration, the landscaping, and the museum itself, and the whole project was incredible. Windsor sounded like the classic rich man with more money than sense.

"Now I understand why Walt was so fascinated with this," Greg said. "He was always curious about people who seemed—well, a little different."

"As I said, I've met Mr. Windsor," she replied. "People don't get much more different than he is."

Greg stared again at the dolmen, silent for a moment.

"You apparently know something about these monuments, or whatever you'd call them," Julie said. "Care to enlighten me?"

"I know a little about English legends," Greg said. "Dolmens are haunted by about five different entities, depending on which legends you choose to believe. Usually, when archaeologists poke into one, they find the body and the grave goods had been stolen a long time ago."

"Windsor said something about that. He emphasized he wasn't disturbing a real tomb because it had been plundered centuries before he came to own it." She checked her watch. "They'll be closing in a little bit. With all the trouble, they check pretty carefully for any stragglers."

"Let's not straggle, then."

* * *

They passed once more through the knot of protesters. Someone tried to stick a leaflet in the rear windshield wiper, but it fell off. Soon, they were headed back into the city.

"It sounds like the British government may solve Mr. Martin's problem," Greg said as they cruised back down the freeway in the gathering dusk. "If they take back the dolmen, wouldn't that sort of gut the museum?"

"If they get around to criminal charges and extradite Windsor, that would do it even more thoroughly. He seems convinced he can hold out legally, but he hasn't got a leg to stand on. It might be that the best we can do is to tie this thing up until he dies."

"Didn't he break U.S. law, too if it was all mislabeled?"

"Yes, but Immigration and Customs Enforcement has more

important things to worry about. They're letting the British take the lead."

Julie looked to her right, where the last glow of the sun was vanishing behind the commercial buildings that choked what seemed like nearly the entire land surface of California. "Greg, does any of this mean anything? About—you know—Walt?"

He breathed out a long sigh. "Not to me. Not yet, anyway. Even if people think Windsor's a racist, why kill a writer doing a story on the museum?"

"Maybe Walt knew something," she said, her knuckles whitening on the steering wheel. "I wondered if he'd found out something—like that MAP was planning violence."

"Even if that's true, I can't see them killing him for it. Not unless this guy Martin is a total psychopath."

"Welles says he isn't. He's been arrested in sit-ins and so forth, but he does his fighting in the courts and in the media. In a way, I want it to be him, just so I know who it is and we can make him pay. But I did some research, and now I'm sure it's not him. Martin throws blog posts and press releases, not rocks."

"I'll bet Welles and his buddies are watching him anyway," Greg said. "Which means there's probably no point in bumbling around after him." He yawned. The drug was wearing off, and tiredness always came flooding back when that happened. "I think the smart thing to do is get some rest. Then we can start from the beginning, see if we can look at this thing from all sides."

"I know what you mean about tired. I haven't slept worth a damn since it happened. The psychologist I went to—I didn't want to, one of the partners at the firm insisted—suggested antidepressants. I didn't want them. I wanted to feel Walt's not being here as much as I enjoyed him being here. I suppose that doesn't make any sense."

"There are no rules at a time like this, Julie. Whatever feels right to you is what makes sense."

"I tried some of those over-the-counter sleeping pills a few nights," she said. "They just made me spacey."

She paused, and as he looked at her, he thought he could see wetness forming in her eyes. "The nights are the hardest," she said more quietly. "You will stay at my apartment tonight, won't you?"

"I will, don't worry. I won't leave you till this is over."

"When's that going to be?" she asked wearily.

"I don't know."

Greg looked out the window at nothing in particular as they drove back to the apartments. It was all too crazy. No way to get in or out of that apartment unless you were a little person or a kid. No motive. Just a murder.

At the apartment, Julie insisted he relax on the couch while she fixed dinner. He stared at the ceiling, listening to her moving about. None of this made sense. It was a disjointed, shadowland dream, and he felt like he was sleepwalking through it.

The microwave in the kitchen sounded its cheery little *bing*, and Julie came in with two plastic plates. "Sorry for the ambiance," she said. "You'll notice I haven't learned to cook since college."

"It's fine," he assured her, yawning again as she set the plates on a small round table in the nook that served as a dining room. He ate fast. Whoever prepped the meals for Julie's larder made a decent lasagna, but he couldn't wait to pick up the articles again.

Julie sat beside him on the couch, surfing the satellite channels on the TV without paying much attention. Greg asked her a few more questions about the articles, though he tried not to make her dwell on the details of the killing.

Eventually, he said, "Well, we're not going to get any more done tonight. I guess I'll bed down on the couch."

Julie shook her head emphatically. "Greg, I need you to hold me."

"I'll hold you."

6

E ven when the last hint of the cafergot boost was gone, Greg didn't sleep well. He dreamed restlessly in broken fragments of stories that always seemed to include the dolmen. He awoke several times. On each occasion, he looked at Julie. His company seemed at least to be helping her to sleep. She was curled under a blanket, seemingly insulated from her nightmare-reality.

Finally, he drifted into a more restful sleep, and neither awoke until nearly ten o'clock.

"We still haven't answered any of the big questions," Greg said, nibbling on a defrosted muffin. "We don't know who, why, or how."

"That's a big help. Can you make any guesses?"

He thought for a moment. "Only vague ones—and they may be wrong. Who—someone who wanted to silence him. Why—he found out something probably about that museum or its opponents." He paused. "Windsor didn't by any chance get his money in some questionably legal way, did he?"

Julie shook her head. "We did due diligence when he hired us. He started with inherited wealth from land and coal mines and managed it very well. He sold the mining interests a few years ago before he moved 'across the pond,' but he kept the family lands over there."

Greg shrugged. "Just a thought. Anyway, the biggest question—how. I don't know how. Police work isn't my field, but I can't say I've ever heard of something like this. For that matter, we still don't know if it's possible for anyone of any size to get through those vents. There may be filters or something further inside."

"Walt didn't tell me about anything strange he found," Julie said. "If he thought he was on the trail of a criminal conspiracy, I'd think he would have told me at least."

"Hmm. I can think of three reasons he might not. One would be to protect you. Two would be if he wasn't sure. Either one of those could fit Walt's way of doing things, I think. Three, he might have stumbled on something and didn't even know it. Someone just *thought* he knew it and had to silence him."

"Maybe that third one," Julie said. "I mean, he didn't seem nervous or extra-careful or anything unusual at all before it happened. He didn't act like anything was wrong."

"Walt was a pretty cool guy most of the time, but I agree you should have noticed something. We've got to know more about his research. Welles said they had his notes. Did he maybe have something more on his computer?"

"Walt always copied his stuff. He handwrote notes, and then he'd type them onto that old computer. He used the tablet mostly for taking videos and doing chats. He always kept some stuff on discs. He thought online backups and cloud services weren't secure."

"We need to look at everything." He hesitated. "I doubt Welles will cooperate. Or has he read the disks already or impounded them?"

"One of the detectives looked through the stuff on his hard drive. I had to help him—I knew some of Walt's passwords and so on. Alan told me they didn't find anything. I'm not sure how thoroughly they read the disks, but they didn't take them with them. I put them back in Walt's desk drawer."

"Welles strikes me as the type who might not tell you more than he had to. Can you still get into Walt's apartment?"

"Well, yes," she said. "But you can't just walk in there. It's an active crime scene."

"I don't know what else to do. Like I said, I don't think Welles is going to let us in again."

"Probably not," she admitted. "But I can just see the headlines if a lawyer is arrested trespassing at a crime scene."

"I think we have to look again, Julie. If it's too hard for you, just give me the key."

She shook her head. "I know where everything is."

* * *

Furtively, they approached the door to 512. No one was in the hall. Greg pointed at the door. "The tape's gone."

"They must have stopped back this morning and finished already," she said. "A murder investigation is a big deal—even in this city. They'll sweep the premises until they're sure there's no evidence left to find. Then they'll just turn it back over to the owner. I'll probably hear from the super pretty soon to move everything out."

"Well, if the cops are done with it, then we don't need to be careful," Greg said. He unlocked the doorknob lock and the deadbolt. Wrinkling his nose in anticipation of another experience with that faint death-smell, he opened the door and stepped in.

"Good God," he said.

The apartment had been in relative order the day before, despite the police search. Now, it was a disaster. The refrigerator door swung open, its contents scattered on the floor. The kitchen drawers had also been pulled out and the dishes and silverware dumped. Behind Greg, Julie edged in the door, both hands clenched into fists and held in front of her mouth as if to stifle a scream.

Greg picked up a cleaver from a pile of utensils on the floor. Feeling a little better with the solid weight of the weapon in his hand, he looked back for Julie. She picked up a knife of her own and edged forward, clutching his left arm.

The living room was worse. The large furniture was still in place, but the sofa cushions had been shredded, flecks of foam rubber littering the living room like fake snow on a movie set. Greg felt Julie's fingernails digging into his arm as he pushed back the half-open door to the office.

"Shit," Greg said. Like Julie, he rarely cursed and took some pride in that fact. But there seemed nothing else to say.

The computer had been hurled from the desk hard enough to make a dent in the opposite wall. The file cabinet lay on its side in a mound of torn paper and manila folders. Walt's blue plastic backup disks were strewn around the floor with the rest of the debris.

"Zip disks," Greg said, surprised he hadn't noticed earlier. "Walt still used Zip disks? I didn't even know you could still buy them. The capacity's so damn small."

"He loved that antique computer. One of his hobbies was talking to other 90s Mac lovers. They trade parts and stuff."

"But he did still do work on it."

"Test documents, anyway. Like I said, they looked."

"We need to read all these disks, but let's check the rest of the place first," Greg said.

Julie just nodded and continued to cling to his arm.

The bathroom wasn't bad—just some towels and odds and ends thrown around. The bedroom, though, looked like it had suffered the brunt of the intruders' fury. The mattress of the double bed was ripped open, with cloth padding and twisted springs protruding like the innards of a slaughtered animal. The bedside table was upended, and the china lamp that had rested on it was broken into small pieces. The dresser drawers were lying on the floor, and a mirror over the dresser had been smashed.

"Greg, who could have been here?"

He put an arm around her shoulders and said the obvious. "I don't know." He released her and walked back out into the hallway. He took another look into the office, eyeing the vent in the ceiling.

"What are you looking for?" Julie asked.

"I'm not sure." Greg went on into the office. One of the chairs was undamaged. He grabbed it and set it upright, dragging it under the vent. Then he stepped gingerly up onto the chair and tugged the vent grating loose. He looked hard at the grating, then stepped down and brought it into the bedroom, where sunlight filtered in through the torn draperies.

"Julie, look."

"What is it?"

"Here." He pointed at two of the louvers in the grate. They were slightly bent in the center, with a deep scratch running from front to back. "What do you make of those marks?"

She shook her head, peering closely at the damage. "I don't know. It's like a chisel or something sharp hit it or got dragged across it. What do you think?"

Greg shook his head. "I don't know, either. These scratches look fresh, though. You can see the metal is still bright in the middle. I think this is something for the police lab to look at."

Julie glanced at the hole in the ceiling and shivered.

"Let's call Alan," she said.

"I think we have to," he agreed. "But I want to find something first."

He set the vent grating down and looked around the office. "I saw his Zip disks just had numbers on them. There has to be a list unless the only copy's on his hard drive. Any ideas?"

"Walt would have a paper copy. Check in the holder," she said. "It's right there on the floor now."

Greg crouched over the battered and nearly empty box. Still inside, right at the front, was a folded piece of paper. He reached down and grasped it, holding it clumsily between the knuckles of his first and second fingers.

"I get the impression you're trying not to leave fingerprints," Julie observed.

"Maybe I'm being paranoid since you said the cops are done with the scene, but I'll bet they could still think of some charges if they wanted to. Might as well not add tampering with evidence to the list."

"Fingerprinting technology is pretty good these days," she said. "The sides of your knuckles would probably be enough."

"Thanks a heap." He shook out the paper and looked at it. "Yep, 'Backup Disk List. There's Anglo Museum, disk thirteen. How appropriate." He nudged the paper back into its container. "See if you see a disk labeled thirteen anywhere."

Julie bent over the nearest pile of disks, turning some over with her foot. "Not here," she said. "Of course, whoever broke in might have taken it."

"No, they didn't," Greg said. He lifted a disk off the floor.

He looked around for Walt's Zip drive and found it smashed against the wall. He looked at the disk. "So here's his information. Now, all we need is another working Zip drive, which may be kind of like looking for an 8-track player."

"Actually, the IT guy at our law office has one. He keeps all kinds of outdated computers and drives so he can retrieve old documents."

"Good." He slipped the disk into his pocket.

"Greg, are you crazy? I thought you didn't want to tamper with evidence."

He offered a grim smile. "You've been questioning my sanity for years. I still don't have an answer. So let's get the hell out of here."

* * *

Welles' reaction was every bit as angry as Greg had expected. Fortunately, his urgent desire to see the apartment outweighed any thoughts he had about throwing them in jail.

"You owe me, Counselor," he said. "Maybe we had the tape off, but you knew damn well not to go poking around in there. Now you show me what you're talking about, and don't you dare so much as breathe on anything that might be evidence."

Welles introduced his partner, a quiet, slightly built Hispanic named Gary Fernandez. Greg noticed Welles had on a white shirt again, and Fernandez wore the same. Maybe that was some kind of unofficial Robbery-Homicide uniform.

Greg and Julie followed the detectives to the apartment. They spent almost an hour sifting through the rubble, but neither displayed much interest in the grating scratches.

"We'll send it to the lab, but it doesn't look like much to me," Welles said. He looked around at the destruction. "It's starting to look like there were more keys to this place than we knew about. And by the way, I want yours. Now."

Greg handed over the deadbolt key.

"Did he have any others?" Welles demanded. "Or did you?"

"No," Julie said. "It must be someone with a passkey."

"That's my job to figure out, Counselor. Now beat it. And stay out of this. Got it?"

They nodded as Greg thought of the computer disk he'd left in Julie's apartment and wondered why the detective didn't notice his obvious, cold-sweating nervousness.

"We'll be good," Greg said.

"We're sorry, Alan. Thank you," Julie said, looking a bit nervous herself.

"Uh-huh." The detective's face softened. "Sorry and dumb. I'm going to forget about this because it's understandable how much you want to know who killed your fiancée. Also, because I'll bet the idea came from Genius here, and I'm letting him off as a favor to you."

"Thank you," she said again.

"Be around. I may have more questions."

* * *

In the parking garage, Greg was about to get into Julie's Mustang when he noticed something. "That's funny."

"What?"

"Come around to this side and look at the back tire."

She did. "There's a wet spot on it."

"From what, though?" Greg crouched down and sniffed. "Not gasoline. I thought it looked like a dog had marked his territory, but it doesn't smell like urine either. Just kind of earthy. What the hell."

"On my list of weird and crazy things going on, that doesn't even rate," Julie said. "Let's go."

It didn't take long to reach the offices of Julie's law firm. "Jerry has the old computers in a spare cubicle near the back," she said as they rode up in the elevator. 'We shouldn't need him to read it, right?"

"There's nothing tricky about reading these," Greg said. "I had one with my old Mac in junior high."

The elevator stopped, and the doors slid apart. "Well, here goes," she said. "I hope I can duck everybody."

To her obvious relief, most of the staff was in conference. The receptionist nodded but said nothing. Julie hurried them through the oak-paneled offices to a large room divided into cubicles. "Here we are. I know the general password. These aren't as protected because they aren't connected to any network."

Greg took in the little gray-walled workspace, desk, and shelves piled with old drives, obsolete IBM and HP desktops, an Apple 320 laser printer, an actual dot matrix printer, and a G4-series Macintosh. "Ah hah," he said, picking up a squat blue drive. "If we can hook this to the Mac, we're in business. Good thing my dad had one of these."

Greg booted up the computer, drumming his fingers on the desk while the machine got in order. "OS nine, with two old versions of Word on it. This should do fine."

Minutes later, he brought up Walt's file on the museum. Julie leaned over his shoulder.

"His notes are still pretty disorganized," Greg noted. "Just typed in chronological order—nothing organized or even spell-checked yet." He paged down through the cyber-document. "Here are some interviews, though. One with Mr. Windsor, one with Rob Martin. Let's see what they have to say."

The interviews had nothing to say. Thirty minutes later, Greg's finger was inching toward the shutdown button, and Julie looked around warily.

"I know you don't want to talk to anyone," Greg said. "Might as well be thorough, though, and check this last folder."

The folder was labeled "European Notes." It had two documents. The first was a partial listing of the museum's contents, just a few dozen items. Each had a value range, presumably from Walt's own research.

"He was trying to figure out what some key items were worth, it looks like," Greg said. "I guess that's kind of splashy stuff he wanted to put in his articles."

"Chariot decoration, small bust of Roman woman, twelve hundred dollars," she read. "Short sword (gladius), first century AD, good condition, ninety thousand dollars. Longer sword (spatha), second-third century AD, excellent condition, eight thousand dollars..."

"Spatha just doesn't sound as cool as gladius, I suppose," Greg said.

Julie kept reading. "Sixth-century burial treasure, eleven hundred items, purchased as one lot, estimate five million pounds on the antiquities market, more if broken up and auctioned individually... (LOOK THIS UP)... Gold helmet, Anglo Saxon, dating disputed, good condition, one of only five in the world, estimated auction value nine million dollars...burial ship, fifth century, poor condition, only one in private hands, estimated over one million..."

"Not very organized, no spreadsheet," Greg said. "Still interesting."

"And worth stealing if you knew how to dispose of it," Julie said. "And there's always someone who does. Okay, I've hooked up the printer if you think it's worth having."

"I do." Greg sent over the document. "Last file."

"Huh," he said. "List of sources on European folk creatures. *The Fairy Faith in Celtic Countries. The European Wildman and His Origins.* Wonder what that was about?"

"I've no idea, but like I said, Walt thought like you. Everything that interested him led to five or ten other things that did."

"Well, it doesn't tell us anything right now," Greg said. "Let's get out of here."

"Nothing remotely about criminal activity except maybe that

value list," Julie agreed. "I just can't think of anywhere else he'd have kept anything."

"At the magazine's office?"

"No, he worked from home. Anyway, Alan told me they checked at the office and talked to everybody, so I'm sure the police have anything that was there.

"Maybe we are wrong about the museum being part of this," she added. "I mean, wouldn't whoever broke in have taken this disk?"

"You'd think so. I'm sure the cops did an inventory during the investigation. They'll go through everything again now and try to find out what might have been taken. Which means they'll notice this disk is missing, which means we could send the cops off on the wrong track if we don't give it back. I guess we really are amateurs."

"Julie!" a hearty voice boomed from behind them.

Julie turned, startled. "Oh—Tom—Mr. Cooley—"

Behind her stood a handsome, graying man in a blue three-piece pinstripe suit. "Tom. This is no time to stand on ceremony, Julie," he said, his voice showing what Greg thought was genuine concern. "We've all wondered how you've been holding up."

Greg stood up. "Greg Preston," he said.

Tom Cooley gave him a strong handshake. "You're Julie's writer friend. She mentioned you once or twice." The lawyer grinned slightly.

"Tom is one of the founding partners here," Julie said. "I'm as okay as you'd expect," she added to the attorney. "Greg was helping me—" she gestured at the computer— "just go through some of Walt's notes and things."

"I'm glad she has a friend," Cooley said to Greg. "Julie is one of our superstars, and I'm not just saying that. We let her solo in court earlier than any other associate we've ever had. She always thinks one step ahead." He turned back to Julie. "Is there anything else we can do for you?"

"No. I'll need to be on leave a little longer, though."

"That's fine. You do whatever you need to do. Go away on vacation if you need to—just call Sandy, and she'll see we pay for it. We not only want to keep you here for your skills, but we like you. That goes for the whole firm."

"I know," she said. "Thank you so much."

Cooley glanced at his watch. "Ouch, late for a deposition. Julie, call me or anyone here anytime. We're here for you." The attorney clasped her hand again, nodded to Greg, and hurried off.

"Damn, I really did hope not to see anyone," she said quietly. "I told you everyone here has been great to me. But they all want to help, and they can't. And I feel lousy about that. It's weird."

"Thinking of other people at a time like this is very 'you,'" he said. "But it's all right to think of yourself right now."

She nodded. "You take the printouts, and I'll take the disk. I'll tell Alan I noticed it and picked it up to give to him, but I forgot it in all the chaos."

"You can't honestly tell me you think he'll believe that."

"Do you have a better idea?"

"Never said I did. Let's go."

*　*　*

They returned to Julie's apartment first. "You wait here while I take this down and see if Alan's still at the apartment. I really don't think he likes you."

"Given what we've done so far, I can't say I blame him."

She managed a little smile. "You always did have a way with people. Remember when you tried to talk your way out of that speeding ticket in college and got your car impounded?"

"I have no memory of any such incident."

"I didn't think you would."

*　*　*

Five minutes later, she was back.

"It's good to see you," he told her. "I was afraid Welles was going to throw you in jail this time."

"Don't laugh. I think he only passed on it because he couldn't prove I was lying. That doesn't mean he believed me, though. I think we'd better stay away from him."

"I don't know. I'm starting to think he's getting sweet on you," Greg said.

"For God's sake, don't say that. That's the last thing I need."

"Sorry. Not the first time I've tried for humor at the worst possible moment. To change the subject, what should we do next?"

She settled down on the leaf-patterned sofa, shaking her head. "I was hoping you'd have an idea."

"I don't, but you know my old saying: when you don't know what to do, do anything. I know there's no evidence, but I can't shake the idea of a connection to that museum. It's nice and sunny out today. Let's go have a better look at it."

7

When Greg arrived at the museum once more with Julie, he was surprised to see no protesters. "At the beach," he suggested.

"Day off," Julie countered with a shrug.

With the absence of picket signs, a few more tourists and other visitors had trickled in. Now Greg saw the outdoor section of the museum was a self-guided tour, with bronze plaques strategically placed to guide sightseers.

With the better light present this afternoon, Greg glanced over the other outdoor exhibits. There were several of them, forming a half-circle around the dolmen. A menhir, a single pillar of rock carved from weathered brown stone, rose ten feet tall between the dolmen and the house. Flanking it were sculptures from various periods of English history, including an imposing Celtic stone cross that seemed to be raising its power in opposition to the dolmen's: the new beliefs facing down the old.

"Well, what do you want to see?" Julie asked. "Do you want to look inside?"

"Not yet," Greg said, gazing to the dolmen. "To coin a phrase, that thing gives me the creeps. In the last few years, I've followed people on everything from ghostbusting to Bigfoot hunts. One time, we were way the hell out in the wilderness with no people anywhere, and something kept throwing rocks at us. I still don't know what that was. But what I'm trying to say is I've never been around anything that seemed—well, as *alien* as that dolmen does."

"Like it just doesn't belong here?"

"No, that's not it. It's more like we don't belong around it." He shook his head. "I'm already talking in lines from my books. Let's go inside."

* * *

The museum building proved to be a very impressive piece of architecture, all burnished wood and rich cloth, but housing what Greg thought was an eclectic, maybe even nonsensical, collection of art and artifacts from English and early American history. Weapons, tools, household items, clothing, paintings, and countless other things were arranged room by room in a roughly chronological order. Greg knew enough to recognize that Celtic, Anglo-Saxon, Scottish, Irish, Welsh, and British items were intermixed, sometimes to jarring effect.

The gold helmet Walt had listed in his notes had pride of place in one of the "Post-Roman Britain" rooms, and it was amazing. Most items were loose or under glass, but the helmet had its own case of transparent high-tech plastic with an alarm system embedded in it. The helmet included a full-face protective mask. The mask was hammered, not cast, and small toolmarks told of the work some craftsman had put into it. Greg looked for a long moment into the eye holes and wondered what history the helmet's wearer must have seen.

As they emerged into a broad gallery that ran the length of this wing of the house, Greg voiced his initial impression. "As a wild guess, professional museum-keepers and art historians probably don't think much of this establishment," he said.

"Walt told me the same thing," Julie agreed. "He said Windsor spent big on this collection, and a lot of the pieces here are one of a kind. But there's no real logic in how he picks them."

"That's not very kind of you."

They turned suddenly at the voice behind them. In the subdued light of the gallery stood a slender, white-haired man of medium height. Blue eyes glittered from deep sockets in a drawn, hawk-nosed face. The man wore a well-tailored suit of medium-weight gray wool, something Greg wouldn't have expected anyone to wear in Los Angeles this time of year.

"Mr. Windsor!" Julie exclaimed.

"The one and only," he replied, raising an ebony walking stick in greeting. His British accent was strong, almost exaggerated. "Miss Sperling. I'm sorry you think as you do."

"I was really just telling Greg what the popular opinion was," Julie said. "And, if I remember correctly, you said that such opinions were of no account to you."

"Spoken like a true attorney," Windsor said. He gave her a brief smile, then turned serious. "My condolences on Mr. Rivas' death. He was a talented and pleasant man to talk to—so unlike most writers I've met lately."

"Thank you," Julie said. "Mr. Windsor, this is my friend and Walt's, Greg Preston."

"A writer," Greg said dryly.

The two men shook hands. "I meant no offense," Windsor said.

"None taken." Greg was already more than a little amused by the man. Windsor, he thought, resembled nothing so much as an American actor doing a bad impression of a stereotypical upper-crust Britisher. It had to be an act. The guy had found a personality he liked and submerged himself in the role.

Greg glanced around to verify there were no other visitors in the gallery. "Mr. Windsor, it probably won't surprise you to learn that Walt Rivas' death is why we're here. The police may already have asked this, but have those protesters or anyone else ever actually threatened violence toward you or the museum?"

Windsor shrugged. "I don't think so. Please remember, though, I usually avoid such matters. The true advantage of wealth is the ability to focus on only those subjects you wish to concern yourself with. I can hire people like this lovely lady to deal with other issues."

"I take it the police have talked to you."

He nodded. "Oh, yes. Unfortunately, I had nothing useful for them. If Mr. Rivas's tragic death is related to this museum, I honestly haven't the faintest idea how."

"Julie mentioned there are some very valuable objects here," Greg said. "Could he have stumbled on some plan to rob the museum?"

Windsor looked troubled for a moment. "That theory had not occurred to me. I suppose it's possible. We have hired the best security firm in California, though. I'll speak to them about being even more vigilant. I am a very peaceful man, but I'm not about to let anyone destroy my work, whether it's burglars or those annoying fellows at the gate.

"And it is *my* work, Mr. Preston. You are quite right about the collection. It is not what most archaeologists would call a scientifically selected and organized presentation. It is more of a personal statement of things I believe are significant. I've spent six decades studying the history of the British Isles and the peoples who inhabit them, and I do have my own opinions about what was important to that history."

"Do you have a staff to help you with the purchases?" Greg asked.

"Oh, I have experts to advise me and arrange the transactions, but, in the end, all the items are of my own choosing. That, I suppose, is the second advantage of wealth. One can make one's opinions heard. All this talk of wealth bringing misery is poppycock to make the rich feel guilty, and the poor feel less unfortunate. I came by my money honestly, Mr. Preston. I use it in ways that please me and, in my opinion, advance society. I apologize to no one."

Windsor's aged voice had taken on a surprisingly strong edge. Greg felt he'd had a glimpse of the man's other side. After all, somewhere behind that amusing facade must have been the skillful businessman who had made the money that allowed his current self to indulge in museum-building.

"Why did you choose the dolmen as part of your collection when you knew it would be hard to smuggle here?" Greg asked.

"Ah, the dolmen," Windsor said, smiling again. "Come sit down, won't you?" He motioned them to follow him down the gallery.

"It was not smuggled, as you and so many others put it. It was saved. The area was going to become housing. If I'd left preservation to the professionals, they'd still have been talking when the bulldozers came."

The house had a central, two-story section and two single-story wings. As Windsor led them onward, Greg saw that, while the interiors of the wings had been designed as exhibit rooms and galleries, the main section was homelike. Windsor ushered them into a sitting-room featuring a large multi-paned beveled glass window. Through it loomed the dolmen, dwarfing the other outdoor exhibits.

"Magnificent, isn't it?" he asked. "The dolmen, Mr. Preston, is significant because it epitomizes the great dominating theme of Anglo-American culture: death. The fear of death, the billions we spend trying to postpone death, the religions that promise to help us cheat death, and the desperate need we feel to raise monuments to ourselves so that we will, in some sense, live on after death. This museum is my monument, I suppose, but the dolmen is a far stronger symbol. Look at it. Think of hewing the stone slabs underneath it by hand and raising a mound like that with primitive tools. What a fear of death that people must have had to put in such effort!"

"Fear of death—and monument-building—are hardly unique to Anglo-Americans," Greg pointed out.

"Very true. The Egyptians did have their pyramids, and so on. But nothing in other cultures compares to us. Most Asian cultures and belief systems accept death as nothing more than a turn on the wheel of life. The Africans, at least the non-Anglicized ones, saw so many real and magical threats to their lives you might say they simply stopped worrying about death. They didn't have the time. The Jews celebrate a dead man's life and move on. But we, for all our professed faith in the Christian resurrection, we are terrified of death more than any one else. Is any other culture so concerned about having sons, about passing on names and titles?"

Windsor became more animated as he continued, pacing rapidly to and fro with less and less use of his walking stick. "No, Mr. Preston, Miss Sperling, that mound out there symbolizes our entire culture as nothing else could. Immortality, that's what we crave and cannot have, save by leaving something behind us, whether it be a painting, a family, or a tomb!"

He slowed, looking suddenly tired as his burst of energy seemed to drain from him. "Well, are you ready to have me carted off to asylum?" he asked.

Damn near it, Greg thought. Windsor's confusing and clichéd mélange of anthropology and psychology certainly sounded like the product of a once-sharp mind getting dull around the edges.

"It's your money, Mr. Windsor," he said. "Nothing crazy about spending it the way you want to. I guess the British government begs to differ, though."

Windsor waved him off with one bony hand. "Let them beg. I will tie them up forever. They're just making a show, at any rate. Her Majesty's government has more important things to worry about, like the never-ending personal failings of the royal family. They will forget about me sooner or later."

Julie shot Greg a rueful grin.

"I saw that," Windsor said. His smile was still present, although it looked a bit forced now. "You know the law, my dear, but I know the thickheaded workings of Number Ten Downing Street. The one thing the British government cannot cope with is an adversary as stubborn as they are."

"For your sake, I hope you're right."

"I am. Well, I have other business—or other pleasures, rather—that I should attend to. Any last questions, my inquisitive friends?"

"Just one," Greg said. He cast another glance at the dolmen. "Does having that thing outside your house make you—well, *uneasy* at all?"

Windsor hesitated. "Personally, no. An ancient symbol of death holds no fears for a man who will meet death soon enough in person. That's why the cowards threatening my death from behind a screen name do not disturb my rest. The guards don't like it at night, though. I trust you don't suppose an ancient curse or some similar rubbish is at work in Mr. Rivas' death."

"No, not at all. I'm just curious about the thing. Thank you very much for your time."

"You're both welcome. Come back whenever you wish. Good day for now." He raised his stick again and then tottered out of the room, leaving Greg and Julie to exchange speculative looks.

"Well, is he a weirdo or what?" she asked with a grin.

"Someone should inform that chap *Downton Abbey* is only fiction," said Greg, in what he knew was a bad imitation of Windsor's accent. "You were right when you said I wouldn't believe you if you described him."

She nodded. "This place always makes me think of the old saying that the difference between men and boys is the price of their toys. I guess this is the ultimate toy box. Why'd you ask him that last question about the dolmen?"

"Beats me. I just don't like the thing, Julie. I don't blame the guards for getting unnerved by it at night."

"It is evil-looking," she agreed. "Don't think I'm the crazy one, but do you really think it might be haunted or something?"

"Most hauntings are in the minds of people who see them, I think," Greg replied. "I know of cases that make me wonder, but if you're asking if there could be such a thing as a homicidal spirit of some sort, I've never seen or read of any credible evidence that would make me think there is."

"I don't think so, either, but I guess something like that had already crossed my mind when I called you. Here Walt was poking around this old tomb and next thing, he was murdered in a locked room by someone who didn't leave any clues. I guess when something like this happens, you just want an explanation—even if it's a crazy one."

"Understood. So far, I like the robbery idea. A sophisticated gang planning a heist might have a professional hitman available to pull off a very clever killing. If that is the case, I'm sure Welles and his comrades will sniff it out." He put an arm around her shoulders and squeezed. "I really don't think there's anything more to look for right now. We might as well go."

Back at Julie's apartment, they passed the afternoon and the evening sampling Chinese takeout and reminiscing about college days.

Greg was pleased to notice she seemed more able to talk about Walt now. He listened as she recounted how they'd had only sporadic contact for a while, with Walt working mostly out in Santa Monica, and then started growing closer. He already knew from contact with Walt pretty much how it had happened, but he let her tell it, and it didn't take him long to realize the story put an odd ache in his stomach.

They were still talking at eleven o'clock. Curious about what was considered top news in his old haunts, Greg turned on the local news —KTSG, of course, which introduced itself modestly as "Southern California's Number One in ratings, respect, and trust."

"Good evening," the silver-haired anchorman began, with a somber expression.

"A prominent local activist is dead tonight. The body of the Reverend Robert G. Martin was found just a short time ago in his Los Angeles office."

Greg grabbed the remote, turning up the volume as he stared at the screen. A file photo of Martin was displayed.

"Police say they can't release any details yet, but they are treating the case as a homicide. We were briefly able to interview the man who found Mr. Martin's body. Here's that video now."

Greg and Julie slid off the sofa and perched on the carpet a foot in front of the television.

A thin-faced, visibly trembling Black man appeared on the screen, running one hand through his salt-and-pepper hair. A chyron below him read, "Lee McGraw—Aide to Robert Martin."

"I came by late," McGraw said, his voice as shaky as his body. "We had a community meeting in Watts, and he didn't come. After it was over, I drove by here, and the lights were still on. So I went in, right, and the door was locked, and I unlocked it, and God, there he was, right on the floor..."

"What did you see exactly?" the off-screen reporter pressed.

"You don't wanna know," McGraw said but went on with the answer anyway. "He was right there on his back, and God, it looked like dogs or something had ripped him up, clawed or bit him open like—"

A hand appeared over the lens. "That's enough. Get this out of here," a gruff voice commanded. There was some arguing and a jerky movement of the camera, and then the video ended.

"That's all we have from the scene, obviously," the anchor said. "The police have cordoned off the building and have released no more information as of yet.

"Mr. Martin has been a longtime local activist in several social and economic causes. Most recently, he was the leader of Museums for All People, the coalition protesting as racist the Museum of Anglo-American Culture. Some of you may recall that a writer, Walter Rivas, who had been reporting on that museum, was recently murdered in a still-unexplained crime. A police spokesman insisted there was no reason to think there is any connection between the two killings. We'll keep on top of this story and bring you new developments as they occur."

The anchor went on to a story on city politics. Greg cycled through the other local channels, but no one had any further information.

Breathing heavily, Greg collapsed back onto the sofa next to Julie. "What do you think?" he asked.

"What am I supposed to think?" she demanded. "Walt first, him next—who after that, me?"

Greg could see fear in her eyes, a sight he had never experienced. He embraced her, and she buried her head in his chest.

"It can't be a coincidence, can it?" she asked.

"I don't know. Martin wasn't like Walt. He was a public figure, and anyone who's involved in lots of causes has lots of enemies."

"That reporter said the room was locked. Just like Walt's."

"We don't know what happened. They might just be talking about a doorknob lock the killer closed when he left. As to the body, it does sound like he was knifed, but this was definitely different. Walt was stabbed once—someone killed him quickly and ran. When you get chopped up like Martin—that's personal."

Julie shook her head. "Everything you say makes sense, but it doesn't convince me. I know they're connected, Greg, and I think you believe it, too."

"I just don't know," Greg insisted. "We need to know more about it."

"Greg, no one's going to tell us anything. And the police certainly aren't going to let us in and look for ourselves."

"What about Welles?"

"Come on, Greg. We don't even know if he's assigned to Martin's case."

"Well, you worked with the cops. Would he be?"

She thought a moment. "Well, now that I think about it, he probably is. The division detective bureaus get most murders, but a high-profile thing like this, which might be political, might go straight to Robbery-Homicide. And he said he was on the response squad this week, which means he gets the after-hours calls. But he wouldn't be where we can reach him. He'd be out at the scene. I have a card with this cell number, though."

"I think we have to do something," Greg said. He felt like he'd taken a fistful of cafergot.

"You were the one a while ago saying there was nothing we could do."

"That still may be true, but I have to act like I'm doing something. We need to see Welles in person. I'm sure he'd take your call, but a phone call makes it too easy for him to blow us off if we start asking questions. Do you know where Martin's office is?"

"Walt told me it was down on Normandie. Something called the Community Education and Action Center."

"Then let's go horn in on the action."

8

The Clan...protect the Clan.

The Clan was all they had. The land was strange, the smells were strange, the creatures around them were strange. The Tall Ones were everywhere. They seemed to have only the feeblest senses and died so easily, but their sheer numbers made it imperative to hide from them.

The Clan was scared. The shared thoughts of all, shared even when they were far apart, held fear.

Hide, hide in the Home Place, hide in the Stinking Holes that ran under the dwellings of the Tall Ones. Come out only to look for food. Food, or to kill the most threatening Tall Ones, the ones whose scents stunk close around the Home Place. Must find them alone and kill, and feed quickly if they fed at all.

Protect the Clan...

9

"Well, there's no mistaking the place," Greg said.

They were peering through the windshield of the Mustang at the visual cacophony of flashing red and blue lights clustered around the front of a brownish two-story office building. Traffic was being detoured, and the area swarmed with police. White trucks sprouting antennas and satellite dishes nosed around the periphery of the melee.

"I don't think we're going to get in," Julie said.

"We're here. What the hell? Park this thing."

Julie pressed her face near the windshield, searching as she drove slowly ahead. Finally, she eased the car between the pumps of a closed gas station, a half-block from the crime scene.

They got out and slowly waded through the logjam of vehicles and bodies toward the police barricades. A helicopter fluttered overhead in the darkness, its spotlight probing down like a giant's finger.

They reached a line of orange-striped wooden horses set up to clear a space for the official vehicles to park. Police were posted just inside the palisade.

Greg and the nearest officer locked eyes for a moment. The

flashing lights showed the cop to be a very tall patrolman, mustached Hispanic. He shot Greg a quick warning glare. "No one past this point, sir."

"Is Detective Alan Welles here?" Greg asked.

The cop just glared harder.

Greg started to try again, but Julie grabbed his arm and slid in front of him. "Patrolman, I'm an attorney with information relevant to this case. I need Detective Alan Welles if he's here."

The forcefulness of her voice cut through the clutter enough to startle Greg a bit. It startled the cop a moment, too, but he regrouped. "Wait here," he said, trying to make it a command. He faded back into the other cops.

"Nice work," Greg shouted in her ear.

Julie shrugged. "A cop's a cop. You have to know how to talk to them."

A moment later, Alan Welles appeared. His jacket already looked disheveled, and the detective's beefy face matched it well. "What the hell are you doing here?"

"We think we can help," Julie said, her voice still firm.

Welles hesitated a moment. "Get in here." He gestured to a crack between two barricade horses, and Greg and Julie squeezed through.

"If you two have information, we'll talk," Welles said. "If you're just fishing, you know damn well I can't tell you anything."

"Detective, how was the door locked?" Greg asked.

Welles stared at him in seeming disbelief. "Tell him the facts of life, Counselor," he said to Julie. "I'm going back to work."

"Was there an air-conditioning vent? How big?"

Welles stopped in the act of turning away. He put his face an inch from Greg's, tilting his head up to glare at the taller man. "You are bugging the hell out of me while I'm trying to investigate a murder. You tell me something useful right now, or I will arrest you for jaywalking or whatever else I feel like."

"It was locked," Greg said. "And you think, just like I do, it had to do with the museum. Listen, what if someone meant to rob the place?

What if Walt Rivas and Rob Martin found out something about the plan?"

"I don't need any stupid theories from you. If you watched the news, you know damn well how Martin was killed, and you know no one did that just to shut him up."

"There's a link, and you know it," he pushed. "Call me. I'll be at Julie's."

Welles seemed too angry—and perhaps amazed—to even make good on his threat of arrest. He just turned and stomped away into the circus. The tall cop was right there, appearing almost magically in Welles' place, putting a firm hand on Greg's shoulder to nudge them back out through the barricades.

As he walked reluctantly away from the scene, Greg noticed one distinctive figure standing out from the confusing swirl of movement. A blonde woman about five feet five was giving hand directions to a fellow in front of her with a camera on his shoulder. Greg couldn't see her face, but he recognized Karen Montrose. "That lady seems to be everywhere," he said.

Julie turned to follow his gaze. "Oh, one of those TV blondes?"

"Karen Montrose. I met her on the plane." At that moment, the reporter glanced around her. As she turned toward Greg, he ducked. Instinct told him he didn't need to be recognized here by a reporter, assuming, of course, she would remember him. She'd want to know why he was here and who knew how messy that could make things.

Karen didn't appear to notice him. As she turned back to the camera and launched into her standup, Greg rose quickly and walked with Julie toward the car.

As they approached the Mustang, Julie gave him a puzzled look. "What's going on?"

"What, with the reporter?"

"No, with Alan Welles. What is it you think you can tell him if he calls you?"

"I don't know yet. I don't even know why I said that. I don't know where the pieces lead, but I've decided you were right. The murders are connected."

"You were just saying how different they were. How Walt was just killed quickly while Martin was torn up."

"Yes, but I had the reason wrong. What if Walt wasn't torn up like Martin just because the killer heard you and ran first?"

"That doesn't make sense. What could anyone have against Walt like that?"

Greg leaned against the car and looked back at the cop/media/spectator mob. "Maybe I'm nuts. I know I don't have all the facts. But what the picture looks like to me is that the same killer did these murders, and I think they would have looked the same if you hadn't come along when you did. And what it's leading me to think about now is less of a normal robber or gang and more of some kind of homicidal maniac. Someone clever, totally insane, and obsessed by something about that museum."

"Greg, come on. A minute ago, it was a robbery. Now you're jumping to a whole new conclusion based on absolutely zero evidence."

He shrugged. "Best I can do."

* * *

In Julie's apartment, away from the adrenaline of the crime scene, Greg wondered about his own leap of thinking. They discussed every aspect of the two crimes without getting anywhere, but Greg found himself unable to stop. They looked at internet news services, saw the same short blurb repeat on MSNBC and CNN, and listened to the all-news radio station repeat the same information.

Finally, Julie switched off her computer. "Let's try to get some rest."

Greg started to follow her into the bedroom. Then he stopped, glancing into the open door of the office. He looked up at the ceiling vent.

"What's wrong?" she asked.

"I don't know. Just—something. Something I don't like about that vent."

Julie looked at him closely. "Greg, I'm the scared one here, remember?"

"Yeah. But let's be paranoid. Do you have the key handy to lock this?"

She nodded. "I'll get it." She paused a second. "You know, you were always the calm one. I don't think I've ever seen you nervous like this."

"I don't think I've ever been like this."

Greg slept badly again. This time, the nightmares were about somebody crashing into the apartment through the ceiling and grabbing him by the throat while he lay there, paralyzed. He woke up shaking, his forehead lined with sweat.

He glanced around in the darkness and shook his head. Weird, he thought. He never had really bad dreams. He couldn't remember one since college.

He looked at Julie in the dim light that filtered up from the street and through the curtains. She was making quick movements, her arms jerking like she, too, was dreaming of unpleasant things. She had pushed the sheets down to her waist, exposing a pink sleep shirt like a knee-length T-shirt, emblazoned with a fading portrait of Garfield the cat saying something funny.

Greg watched the irregular rise and fall of her breasts under the fabric. Then he looked at her face—troubled even in sleep, beautiful even when troubled.

Old feelings are like old soldiers. They never die. They just fade away. But anything that's not dead can come back...

No. Not now. She needs a friend, not a goddam vulture coming in trying to rewrite our history.

Finally, he sank back on the pillow. He'd almost made it when Julie jerked upright, her eyes flying open, gasping in fear.

"Greg!" she shouted, looking around wildly.

Shaking wide awake, he grabbed her and clutched her tightly, both arms wrapped around her trembling body. "It's okay. Okay. I'm here. You were just dreaming."

Still shaking, she nodded. "I know. It was just so real. Walt was buried under that tomb, that dolmen thing—buried alive, and I couldn't get to him." She brushed tears from her face. "Sorry, I'm such a helpless female right now. Good thing I'm not in court, huh?"

"Julie, we all have bad dreams." He rubbed her back and neck with one hand. "Right now, you're certainly entitled to yours." For some reason, he glanced at the glowing numbers of the clock on the nightstand. Four-thirty-one.

"I've had them all night," she said. She pulled back from him a little, brushing her disheveled hair from her face. "Before that, I dreamed I was here, and something was breaking in—"

"You dreamed that?"

"I just said I did."

"So did I," he said, gripped by a sudden chill he'd never felt before. "Julie, what—"

She dug her nails into his arm. "What's that?"

He listened. It sounded like movement. Movement somewhere in the ceiling.

He turned to Julie. "Get the hell out of here!"

An instant later came a thud, and he knew what it was. It was a vent grating being dropped to the floor.

Julie didn't hesitate. They bolted out of the bed, then out the bedroom door, and their four hands frantically turned the deadbolts to the apartment. Greg slammed the door behind them as they turned and ran down the hall toward the elevator. He jabbed the button repeatedly, looking over his shoulder at the scary emptiness of the hall behind them.

The elevator arrived after what felt like an eternity. They tumbled into it and shut the doors. Julie hit the button for the lobby, and they clung to each other as the car slid down the shaft.

"Oh God, Greg, who's in my apartment?"

"Don't know," he gasped. "But I want to let the cops find out, not us."

The elevator slid to a stop. The moment the door opened, they tumbled out into the main lobby and rushed through it into the outer. The night guard looked up, startled, as a nightshirt-clad woman, who he recognized as a resident, and a man in a T-shirt and gym shorts ran up to his podium as if pursued by the devil himself.

"Call the cops!" Greg snapped. "Now!"

The guard, a stout man who looked like a military veteran with short, reddish hair and heavy eyebrows, shot each of them a glance. "Miss Sperling, right? What's going on?"

"Julie Sperling, seven oh four, yes," Julie stammered. "Someone just broke into my apartment. They're still in there."

"One person or more?" the guard asked.

Greg had the thought that if he said one, the guard would go up by himself, and he had an overwhelming feeling the guy would get killed. "Two. I heard two."

The guard flipped up a protective cover, typed for a moment on a keypad, and hit a red button.

"Okay," he said firmly. "Cops will be here in a second. Let's start from the top and get a story. Names first." Definitely ex-cop or ex-military, Greg thought.

They were still trying to get it straight when the guard saw movement in his monitor and buzzed in the LAPD. Two officers, a stocky Black three-striper and a nervous-looking white rookie type, hurried in.

"What have you got, Sarge?" the older cop asked.

"Glad it's you, Dex," the guard said. "Miss Sperling and her companion report at least two people broke into her apartment. Number seven oh four." He already had a card and a passkey in his hand. "They came running like hell down here."

Dex frowned. "How could anyone get in without coming through here?"

"I dunno, but I know Miss Sperling here. If she says somebody did, I'd check it out."

"Okay," the officer said. "Wylie, let's take the elevator. Sarge, lock the stairwell. You got a portable?"

The guard pulled a walkie-talkie from a rack under his podium and handed it to the officer.

"Okay. Anything comes down the stairs, you yell. Till then, get our witnesses somewhere safe and sit on 'em. Let's go."

The cops headed up. Greg and Julie watched them go, still breathing heavily, trying to calm themselves down.

"Why don't you two go in the office there," the guard said, pointing to a narrow door marked *Employees Only*. "I'll keep an eye on things out here."

For long minutes, Greg and Julie huddled on a tiny couch in an equally diminutive office that appeared to belong to the security manager for the apartment building. Neither spoke. Both watched the door.

They jumped when it opened. It was the LAPD sergeant.

"I think you two better come up here," he said.

* * *

A quick ride up the elevator, and they were following the cops back into the apartment. Greg felt a wave of uneasiness despite the presence of two armed officers plus the security guard. *Some macho hero you are*, he thought.

There was no visible damage to the door or the kitchen. The office was a different story.

"Oh, God," Julie breathed.

The door hung open on one hinge. The deadbolt was intact, but the door had been hit so hard from the inside that it was splintered vertically almost in half.

The young cop looked in, then motioned to his partner. "Must have got in through that ceiling vent," he said.

Dex shook his head. "Maybe if they were real small. But how'd they get in there to start with?"

"Officer, do you know Detective Welles from Robbery-Homicide?" Greg asked.

"Heard of him."

"I think you'd better call him."

* * *

About half an hour later, a red-eyed Welles rumbled in through the lobby door, Fernandez right behind him. The smaller detective also looked tired but was still so fluid in his movements that Greg wondered if he was a martial art adept of some type.

"Sorry to drag you guys in," Greg said.

Welles waved it off. "Not like we expected any sleep tonight anyway. Counselor, are you all right?"

Julie, now a little more composed and with a T-shirt and jeans on, nodded. "We're fine."

"Good to hear. Now, what's up? Dispatch didn't say much except you had a break-in."

"That," Greg said, "is one hell of an understatement. You'll want to take a look at Julie's apartment."

Welles shrugged. "Lead on."

* * *

After a brief discussion, the detectives released the two patrol officers and followed Greg and Julie into the apartment.

"Somebody sure doesn't like you very much," Welles said, eyeing the smashed door.

"Take a look at how they got in," Greg said. He pointed to the grating. Welles and Fernandez bent over the evidence, Fernandez pointing out scratches and dents in the louvers.

"It looks like the damage to the one in Mr. Rivas' apartment, but much more violent," Fernandez said. "Maybe this time, the intruder was more interested in speed than in doing things covertly."

"Door sure bears that out," Welles agreed. Fernandez had already pulled out a cell phone and was using its camera to take a close-up of the grating.

"You said you sent that grating from Walt's apartment to the lab," Greg said. "What did they say about it?"

Welles shook his head. "SID didn't get to it yet, as far as I know."

"Evidence in a murder case, and they didn't get to it?"

"Mister Preston," Welles said, drawing out the title with an aggravated tone, "do you have any idea how many murders the Scientific Investigation Division lab is working right now?"

"No."

"Lots. More than they can possibly cope with as fast as you'd like —or as fast as I'd like, for that matter. Now exactly where were you two when this happened?"

"Asleep in the next room," Greg said.

"I see." Welles gave Greg a questioning glance, the exact meaning of which Greg wasn't sure about, and switched it to Julie for just a moment.

"And the noise woke you up?" Welles continued.

"Actually, we were awake," Greg said. "This sounds kind of melodramatic, but we both had nightmares about somebody breaking in here. That's what woke us up. We were awake when we heard it. That was a little after four-thirty."

Welles rubbed the shadow on his chin with one hand. "Let's go sit down."

* * *

Julie brought in coffee and tea in the living room of the apartment. Both cops took black coffee. Greg had never liked coffee more than tea, so he rummaged in the fridge and found a diet cola for his caffeine fix.

The detectives produced notebooks and a phone with a recording app and took their statements methodically, one at a time, while the other waited in the bedroom. When that task was out of the way, Greg had a question of his own.

"Since you've been up all night, I take it there's still a lot to be done on Rob Martin. Am I right?"

Welles exhaled noisily. "He never quits, does he, Counselor? Just to shut you up, no, there's a lot we don't know. I will tell you he was in his office. Yes, the door was locked, but it was just a doorknob lock. Anyone who killed him could have locked it behind him."

"How'd the killer get in, though?"

"Not sure. The main door was locked. There was an open second-floor window someone with agility could have climbed through. Or it could have been someone with a key, which we're obviously running down now."

"What was he killed with?"

The detectives exchanged glances, Fernandez shaking his head.

"Look," Welles said. "You guys are scared, and we want to solve this whole mess. I'm willing to give you some details if I think they'll help, but that's my call, not yours. I can't go any further unless you come across with something to help me first."

Fernandez gave Welles a quick look, which Greg intercepted. The younger cop was surprised Welles had told civilians anything.

"Damn it, I don't have anything—yet," Greg said. "If we're going to put this together, we need all the pieces on the table. Look, just tell me this. What was the murder weapon? And was that witness right? Was he torn up like somebody had really hated him, wanted to make it as bad as possible? Or like an animal had done it, I think he said?"

"The witness was right about how messy it was," Welles said. "We don't know about the weapon. Yeah, he was ripped up worse than any vic I've ever seen. I even thought about a trained animal, but it was more likely just a knife with a lot of rage behind it."

"I can't believe you're still unsure," Greg said. "A knife doesn't look like animal claw marks, not that much. The coroner must know what it was by now."

"You seem to think you're the cop here," Welles said. "Let me remind you that you're not. But while you're playing detective, answer me this. We know Walt Rivas was killed with a knife," he went on, with a glance of sympathy toward Julie. "If you're so sure the murders are connected, why are you hinting it wasn't a knife with Martin?"

"Sure, I'm speculating," Greg said. "But the same killer might use different weapons. In Walt's case, the knife was right there, handy. In Martin's case, it wasn't."

"What, there was no knife, so the killer goes out and gets a Doberman? Suppose you're right, and it wasn't a knife. What would that prove?"

"Do you know of any murders done with animals?"

"Hell, yeah. I arrested a guy once who set a pit bull on a neighbor who played his stereo too loud. The dog ripped out his throat. Now, once more. Assume someone killed Martin with an attack dog or whatever. What's that prove?"

"Think about what we've got here," Greg said. "One case where a killer, who must have been small and agile, entered through a ceiling vent and stabbed a man. One where a killer probably climbed through a window and ripped a man apart, with weapons unknown. A few hours later, someone busts in here through the ceiling vent and would have killed us if the office door wasn't locked. And the only thing tying it all together is that museum or something about it."

"You're still making several suppositions," Fernandez said. "We can assume the first and third events are connected, but it's still conjecture that the Martin killing is. I suspect Miss Sperling could dismantle your arguments in a courtroom."

"I probably could," Julie said. "But that's what I think, too."

"Look, Genius, cut to the chase." Welles' puzzled look was morphing into one of serious aggravation. "Where is all this leading you to?"

Greg shook his head. "It all reminds me of something I can't believe. But I need to get to the library first—some of what I want won't be online. Without research, you'll say I'm crazy. And I might very well agree with you."

"If you're holding back something, I'll bust your ass for it."

"I just don't have a coherent theory yet, Detective," Greg said. "I've got some pieces that remind me of things I only half remember reading. Look, can we come see you later on today?"

"And what will you tell us then?"

"Maybe that I was full of crap all along, which I'm sure is what you think now. But I don't think you've got a theory that fits all the facts, so you might as well let me try to come up with one, no matter how insane. God knows I'm not trying to get in your way. You've got two people here—" he made an inclusive gesture toward Julie— "who are scared to death. We want to know who or what came after us tonight and how we can help you solve this before we get murdered."

Julie made a little sound in her throat. Greg instantly regretted his phrasing but knew she'd been thinking the same thing.

Welles flung up his hands. "I give up. Counselor, where did you get this guy?"

Julie actually smiled a little. "He's an old friend. That's why I signed him out of the psych ward. Don't worry, he's in my custody."

"Uh-huh."

"You're not a fan of Poe, are you, Mr. Preston?" Fernandez asked.

"Huh?"

"Edgar Allen Poe. He wrote *The Murders in the Rue Morgue*. A story about murders committed by a trained ape."

"I'd forgotten all about that—honest," Greg said. "But that doesn't mean it's out of the question."

"I can't believe I'm having this conversation right now," Welles said, shaking his head. "Look, we're going to check with the neighboring apartments, and then we're out of here. I'll have a team come over and go through the evidence. Check for prints on the door, figure out what it was hit with, that kind of stuff. If you got something for us, come downtown this afternoon and ask for us. You know where we are, Counselor."

"One thing's for sure," Julie said. "I'm not staying here any longer. Can I just leave you keys?"

"Sure. I was about to suggest that. Find a hotel or something, maybe at least a few miles away. Someplace you've never even visited, just in case the perp knows something about your habits. Just let me know where you are."

They packed quickly as Welles and Fernandez waited for their relief and tried to stay awake. With a promise to keep in touch, they grabbed their bags and headed out.

In the elevator, Julie slumped against the wall. "He was right when he used the word 'insane.' This is insane, Greg. It's all insane. I'm insane."

"No," Greg said. "Someone or something else is insane."

"Are you going to tell me what you think it is?"

"I'll tell you. But first, let's find that hotel."

10

At Greg's suggestion, they called a cab, hoping that would make things more difficult if someone were stalking them and looking for Julie's car. A police officer stayed with them until the cab came.

Julie knew of a newly remodeled and reopened hotel on Figueroa Street, on the southern edge of L.A.'s booming central high-rise district. When they arrived, Greg asked for an upper-story room. He drew a puzzled glance from the desk clerk when he asked to inspect the room first, but she obliged him.

It looked good. All the air-conditioning vents were small, and no patios or balconies would make the glass walls climbable. "This'll do fine," he said.

They settled in and ordered breakfast delivered. It was just after seven AM.

"Greg, can they—whoever—find us here?" Julie asked, sitting on the edge of the bed.

"I don't know. We took some precautions, but I can't say for sure we weren't tailed."

"Tailed by who? Or what? You promised to tell me, remember?"

Greg paced to the window and looked over the city from their eighth-floor vantage point. "Julie, I don't know. There's only one thing I can come up with, and I don't believe it. Walt's folklore sources made me wonder. I thought he was just trying to add context to his museum stories, but maybe not. Maybe he heard something about something crazy and was trying to figure it out."

His pacing took him back beside the bed, and Julie grabbed his arm. "Damn it, what are you talking about?"

He hesitated, then took the plunge. "Do you know what a korrigan is?"

"I have no idea."

"Let's see if I can find something to show you." Greg unpacked his laptop and found the room's internet connection. Ignoring the signals that told him he had mail, he started calling up search engines and punching in the word "korrigan."

After ten minutes, he gave it up. "Nothing useful," he said. "A lot of mentions from role-playing games and what seems to be an article on folklore, but it's in French. We're going to have to do this the old-fashioned way."

"Do what?" she demanded.

He glanced at his watch. "Library opens in two hours."

* * *

Greg set his watch alarm, and they managed a nap on the room's king-sized bed. Then, they forced themselves to get up and planned the day ahead. Julie joined him in selecting jeans, pullover shirts, and athletic shoes from their luggage. They took a cab and went uptown a few blocks to the massive, temple-like Los Angeles County Main Library.

* * *

After three hours of research, a forgettable lunch from a tiny sandwich shop, and some talking in their room, they called an Uber.

Their destination was LAPD headquarters in the Police Administration Building, in the middle of downtown.

Greg knew the old police building, the iconic Parker Center, from a TV show his parents had liked when he was young. He'd always thought the PAB didn't have nearly as much character. It was handsome in its way, all glass, concrete, and steel, with a plaza leading into an airy lobby. Remove the police emblems and flags, though, and it could have been any big corporate headquarters. Those cops on *Hunter* would never have recognized it.

Greg gave his name at the entry desk and asked for Welles, and the cop on duty nodded.

"He's expecting you. Stand by just a minute."

Fernandez appeared and signed them in, and they followed him into a wood-paneled elevator and up to the RHD lair on the fifth floor. They entered a huge office space, all aluminum-framed glass reaching a high ceiling, with generic modern cubicles, desks, and file cabinets all over the place. About half of the desks were occupied by detectives, mostly men in white shirts.

Welles stood up to greet them. Without any small talk, he led them to a tiny, glassed-off meeting room. "Okay, Genius," Welles said as he settled heavily into a chair. He looked like he hadn't been to bed since the gunshot in the hotel. "What've you got?"

"First, I've got a name. Preston, Gregory Arthur. Pick any one of the three."

Welles chuckled. "Okay. I know that habit of mine drives some people crazy. What've you got, Greg?"

"Before I sound insane, let me ask if you've turned up anything that makes it sound like this really is an ordinary series of crimes by an ordinary person. Anything new on Martin?"

Welles sighed. "Not a damn thing. As a matter of fact, the only reason I figure you're worth talking to again is that we're making zero progress." He hesitated. "I guess you're deep enough in this mess to trust you. I've trusted you a lot already, not that you've earned it," he said with a sharp glance at Greg. "If I'm going to share any more details, I need your promise you'll keep everything you've heard from me confidential."

"We promise, Alan," Julie said. "For that matter, if anybody asks me, I can always set things up so Greg's my client, and it's privileged."

"They miss you in the DA's office." Welles grinned. "Anyway, it's like I said. I'm willing to hear your theory because I haven't got one of my own. Rob Martin was last seen alive before eight. The aide who saw him last left him there alone. He thinks the office door was closed, but he's not sure. There were no marks on the air-conditioner vents, which are really small anyway. Best guess is the suspect entered that second-floor window, even though they didn't leave ladder marks, and went into Martin's office down the hall through the door.

"Despite the damage done to the body, there were no signs of struggle. We can't be sure, but it looks like he got taken by surprise. Martin's shoes had been untied and removed, apparently by him. Best guess is he'd just put his head on his desk to catch a few winks and maybe slept through that meeting in Watts that he missed."

"Describe the wounds, please," Greg said.

Fernandez opened a manila envelope. "Miss Sperling, you might not want to look at these," he warned in his usual accented but precise English. "As Alan remarked last night, this is the most violent murder we have ever seen."

Greg picked up the first photo, an 8x10 glossy that looked like it had been taken on good old-fashioned film. His stomach knotted up at the first look.

Martin's body had been gutted. It looked like a grizzly bear had torn his chest and abdomen apart. Shredded organs were spilled out haphazardly, and a dark stain of blood covered the body and the adjacent floor.

Greg glanced at Julie. She'd turned distinctly pale and averted her eyes from the photo.

"I never saw anything like this, except maybe on *CSI* or a horror movie," Greg said. "I remember a picture of a man who'd been killed in Kenya by a leopard cult that tore his heart out. It was nowhere near this bad."

"Nothing was missing from the office," Welles said. "Martin's files and computer were untouched. His wallet was in the desk, money and credit cards still inside."

"Is the body—you know, all there?" Greg asked.

"Initial coroner's report says no body parts were removed or eaten," Welles said. "It says something else, too. Says their first guess about a weapon was animal claws. But they haven't been able to match it up to anything yet." He glanced at a battered little brown notebook. "Left four parallel gashes on some parts of the body but doesn't look like a dog's or a big cat's paw."

"Something exotic, maybe," Greg said. "A wolverine or something like that?"

Welles shrugged. "Coroner had a guy over from the zoo this morning to look at the claw marks. Said he had to study them some more. By the way, there were no teeth marks. Just the claws."

"Have them check for metal fragments in the wounds," Greg suggested. "That African cult I just mentioned—the leopard men? They made steel claws that fit over their hands. Supposedly, they only existed in Africa, and they were wiped out seventy years ago, but I suppose anything's possible in LA."

"Sounds good, but does it explain how they got through the little air vents?" Welles asked.

"No," Greg said. Then he grinned. "This is interesting. I just thought of a plausible explanation—well, kind of plausible, anyway —and you were the one who shot it down. Were there any other clues as to who or what may have done it?"

Welles consulted his notebook again. "Some funny puncture marks in some of the bones. Breastbone, both hips, upper legs. Like the animal jabbed a claw or tooth in so hard it cracked open the bone."

Greg let out a long breath. "If you hadn't just said that I don't think I'd have the nerve to tell you this," he said. "I'm going to sound ridiculous, even to me. But if it was an animal, and the wounds don't match anything known, then I do have the beginnings of a theory."

Welles glared like Greg was a small but offensive bug he was about to stomp. "One warning. If you say this is a werewolf, Dogman, or wendigo, I will shoot you myself."

Greg raised his hands. "Absolutely not. Those are fantasy creatures, nothing else."

"Okay, so I won't shoot you yet. So let's hear your bright idea of yours."

Greg pushed back his chair and stood up. "Old habit," he said. "I think better on my feet." He began to pace the little room, talking as he went.

"Fact number one: Walt Rivas was stabbed in his apartment. The only apparent way in or out was through the air-conditioning vents—vents no one larger than child-size could get through.

"Fact number two: contradicting fact number one, the stab wound required the strength of an adult male.

"Fact number three: something broke into Julie's apartment this morning. This time there was no question it used the air vent."

"We know the facts," Welles interjected. "Is there a point in here somewhere?"

"Give me a break," Greg said. "Maybe I'm trying to convince myself. Just humor me.

"Fact four: Walt and Martin were both poking around that museum and the dolmen.

"Fact five: Martin was apparently torn up by an unidentifiable animal that climbed in through the second floor."

He took another deep breath. "So if the same suspect committed all the crimes, here's his profile. Size: three to four feet tall. Strength: equal or better than a man. Hands with sharp claws but with the dexterity and intelligence to use a knife. Smart enough to track people and find its way through ducting to a desired room. Finally, has some connection to British history."

"So, are we back to Gary's idea about the story with the trained ape?" Welles asked.

"Detective, no animal fits that description. It's like a chimp with claws, but a chimp's not murderous. Maybe you could train one to kill —I'm not sure, ask your zoo guy—but there's no way a chimp did that to Martin. So where does that leave us?" Greg felt himself sweating despite the crisp temperature the air conditioning had imposed on the room. Welles' brown eyes and Fernandez's black ones were looking at him with profound skepticism—and he hadn't even broached his theory yet.

"I don't believe I'm saying this. You don't have to tell me I'm crazy because I already know." Greg felt warm all over. "But I just can't think of anything else that fits. I keep coming back to the museum. Specifically, the dolmen.

"According to English legend, dolmens are the haunts of something called korrigans. There are several completely different versions of what a korrigan looks like, but the one that matters is that a korrigan is an evil dwarf. Not a dwarf like the old term for short people, or like *Lord of the Rings*. A humanoid animal. Dark and hairy, with black eyes and with talons on its hands.

"That legend is found all over England and in Brittany. Korrigans supposedly lived in caves and mines as well as burrowing into dolmens."

Welles snorted, shaking his head. He seemed too stunned to be truly angry as he turned to Julie. "Counselor, what is your buddy here high on? Something I can arrest him for, I hope. Shit, I'd have liked it better if he said a wendigo."

"I told you it was crazy," Greg said evenly. "And I don't even say I believe it. I'm outlining an idea here. A speculation. If you don't have a better one, let me finish."

Welles started to say something, apparently failed to find the right words, and shrugged yet again. Fernandez gave Greg the look an officer might give a street corner lunatic shouting about the Second Coming.

"All right," Greg said. "First question: do korrigans exist?

"To begin with, there's the legend itself. As I said, it's all over

England and Brittany. Like the dolmens itself, it dates from before the time of Christ—no one's sure how far back it really goes.

"More to the point, there are other stories that get more specific. Miners all over Europe have reported beings like this further underground. Used to report them, anyway. The Germans called them kobolds. The Vikings developed a mythology about Hadding Land—a subterranean world peopled by black dwarves.

"In the spring of 1138, the monks at Brumia Monastery in the Trier region of Prussia captured a dwarf in their wine cellar. He'd broken in from a hole that seemed to the monks to go down forever.

"The only description of him in the story, recorded by a monk named Gervase, is that he was dark-skinned. He refused food and drink, seldom slept, and never spoke. Finally, he ran back to the cellar, attacked the winekeeper, and escaped. The monks sealed up the hole."

"Then there are what people call the goblin-holes. All over Europe. They date back to the Middle Ages and beyond—some to the Neolithic. There are passages in them as small as eighteen inches. And they're swept clean. There are no artifacts in them. No feces. Archaeologists can't explain them. But a race of small, tunneling creatures, who were once widespread but now extinct, or almost extinct? That would explain them.

"It might explain all the stone dolmens in the Caucasus, too. They're made of stone, about a meter high, with an opening like a hobbit-hole closed with a stone plug. The folklore is that they were built by or for an ancient race of dwarfs." He paused as a fresh thought struck him. "Archaeologists have always assumed the plug was to keep people out. Maybe it was, at least sometimes. Or maybe it was to keep something in."

Greg was talking fast, constantly expecting one of the cops to break in to tell him he was being committed and the interview was over. He was surprised when Fernandez raised a hand politely, as if in a lecture class.

"Just a moment, Mr. Preston," the usually silent cop said calmly. "Assume, just for the moment, that there actually is an unknown animal, an apelike creature, behind these legends. If they exist, where have they been for hundreds of years?"

"Well, this is pure conjecture, but I have an idea there, too," Greg said. "The sightings and legends come from all over, but the greatest number, and the most recent ones, come from Britain. Say these things liked Britain, for whatever reason, and eventually, that was where the only real population made its home. A thousand years ago, the climate in the British Isles was much warmer than it is today. Then it started changing. Maybe the korrigans just couldn't take the cold."

"And what?" Welles asked, his tone more derisive. "They hibernated like Smoky the Bear?"

"No, I don't think so. Remember, that whole dolmen was dug up, crated, and reassembled. Full-grown korrigans couldn't have been overlooked. But they might have missed anything smaller than that if they were just taking big backhoe chunks of the dirt at a time."

"Like what?" Julie asked.

"Say they're not just like little people. Maybe they're so different from us they lay eggs. Water flea eggs have been hatched after being dormant for seven hundred years. Or maybe their babies can go into something like cryptobiosis."

"Crypto-what now?" Welles snapped.

"There are little insect-like creatures called tardigrades that do it," Greg said. "If the environment is too hostile, first they curl up like armadillos, then they lose all the water in their bodies and become even more compact suspended-animation forms called tuns. They don't need moisture or even oxygen. Tardigrades in the tun state have survived when taken to the International Space Station and exposed directly to the vacuum. When the environment is more benign, even if it's years later, they come back to life."

Finally, Welles snorted and said what Greg was expecting him to. "No," he said. "No more of this. This is just too nuts, and that's the nicest word I can think of. Bullshit is a lot better word."

"Do you have a better theory?" Greg asked.

"It's not about better," Welles said, looking him firmly in the eye.

"It's about possible and impossible. Some killers are clever. Some are smarter than me. What we have here is one who's outsmarted us so far. What we do not have here are little monsters that don't exist."

"Fine. Fine, Detective. You can listen to my crazy ideas, or you can—"

Greg stopped as the door opened.

A young uniformed officer, a wiry Black man, rushed in. "Detective Welles, I'm sorry to interrupt, but you wanted to know anything that happened at that museum."

"What is it?"

"A Mr. Tom Windsor has been reported missing."

11

Welles gave Greg a long look.

"Well, Genius, looks like the fairy tales will have to wait." He turned back to the edgy-looking young cop. "What's the report?"

The officer looked at the screen of his cell. "Detective, one of Mr. Windsor's assistants, or whatever, called us. Seems he went out for an early morning walk. The guy said he always does that. When he didn't come back, they checked the whole estate and couldn't find him. I know we don't usually jump on a missing-persons report this soon, but like I said, anything to do with that museum—"

Welles waved him off. "All right. Good job, Bates. Let's get our asses out to the estate."

Greg raised his eyebrows when the officer mentioned Welles's interest in the museum. Julie had been right on that score. "Alan— Detective Welles—could we—"

Welles nodded. "All right. You know your way around that place, and you saw him yesterday. You might know something useful. You keep quiet and do as you're told. Got it?"

"Deal."

* * *

Welles' unmarked blue CRV zoomed toward the Windsor estate. The detective had put a flasher on his roof and now was weaving in and out of freeway traffic. "Morons," Welles said, hunching over the steering wheel. "Some of these people wouldn't get out of the way if we were a tank."

Actually, Greg thought, people were clearing out as well as they could, but mentioning that seemed like a bad idea.

A husky sergeant met them at the gate. "Nothing found yet, Detective," he said. "We've got people looking all over the place."

"Thanks," Welles said. He drove in and squeezed the unmarked car into a spot between two black-and-whites. "Gary, see who's in charge here." He turned to Greg. "Tramping over the same ground everyone else is looking at isn't going to do any good, so let's start from another direction. I want to see this tomb thing that fascinates you so damn much."

The group left the car. They dodged museum personnel searching the grounds, accompanied by LAPD patrol officers in their dark blue uniforms. Fernandez went into the museum building while the others kept going. Along the way, they picked up a young cop named Poole, a blond surfer type with a narrow face and odd, almost pointed ears. Greg thought momentarily of one of Tolkien's elves, something which didn't seem at all out of place at the moment.

Poole gave them a quick rundown on who was searching and where. Greg led the group around the museum building to the dolmen.

Welles studied the monolith for a few minutes, pacing back and forth and looking from different angles while no one spoke.

"It's a creepy-looking thing, all right," Welles finally said. "I can see why it makes you think about dwarves, goblins, or whatever—even in daylight."

He turned to Poole. "Where did Windsor do his walking?"

"Apparently, he usually walked east, away from this part. He walked up the road to the gate and back. Not very far."

"The road's been covered plenty of times by now," Welles said. "Somebody took him somewhere."

"Or he saw something and went to investigate," Greg said.

"Or ran away from something," Julie suggested.

Welles raised his hands to silence them. "When I want theories, I'll ask—and don't hold your breath. Officer Poole, were there any traces found at all so far?"

"No, sir. We're bringing in a dog team, and they've already got a Hummer up in the rough areas. He sure has a lot of land here for L.A. Chopper's on the way, too."

"Has the area around the dolmen been searched?" Greg asked.

"Once, by the estate people," Poole said. "We haven't concentrated here because we know he started the other way. His butler, or whatever, saw him leave. We'll check it again, of course."

"Let's check it now."

Poole looked at Welles. "Detective?"

"Yeah, let's look around."

The group circled the dolmen. Greg studied the tomb's grassy sides closely, wondering what he was looking for. He did know he felt scared, even in midafternoon and with armed cops around. For the first time, as far as he could remember, Greg wondered whether he was brave. He was like most, he supposed—maybe brave sometimes, not so much the rest of the time. Either way, he wished he and Julie were somewhere else.

Julie kept close to Greg's side. He took a second to study the shaken look on her face. She had voiced the same disbelief the cops had about his idea of the korrigans, but what she'd seen in her apartment had probably thrown her, and now she didn't know what to believe.

"Hey, what's that?" Poole asked.

The patrolman pointed at the base of the dolmen. Where the bottom of a stone slab protruded from the earth, the museum staff had planted some leafy waist-high bushes. What Poole had noticed was an area of disturbed soil under the bushes.

"Could be just gardening work, but let's take a look," Welles said.

Greg was already scrambling behind the bushes. The turf had been removed and inexpertly patted back down in an area about six feet long but narrow. On impulse, he grabbed a piece of the turf and raised it. It came away easily. He dug one hand into the dry soil—and his fingers touched cloth and clammy cold skin.

With a shout, Greg leaped back. He crashed into and over the bushes, rolling away from the spot. As the others gathered around him, he pointed a shaking finger at the dirt.

"Windsor," he gasped. He clutched at Julie as she held him in a tight, soothing embrace.

* * *

A narrow trench had been scooped out, less than three feet deep, and Windsor's body jammed in sideways. The corpse looked like Rob Martin's—torn open as if by a clawed animal.

Welles gave Greg the details as he rested beside the cars, out of sight of the dolmen. After pointing out the grave, Greg's next action had been to throw up. Julie hustled him into a museum restroom and helped him get cleaned up. Greg washed his right hand at least a dozen times in water so hot it scalded him.

Now, he was sitting in the sunlight, his back against Welles' car.

When Welles headed back to the crime scene, Greg turned to Julie. "Not very impressive as an investigator, am I?" he asked. "The first thing I do is lose my lunch."

"If I'd have touched him, I would have lost my mind," Julie offered. "My God, Greg, this thing is unreal. If these things—these animals or whatever—are real, why are they killing everyone?"

"I don't know."

"Can you guess?"

Greg thought for a moment. "If I had to guess, maybe it goes like this. They just woke up, or whatever, a few months ago when the dolmen was shipped to a warm climate. Obviously, they mature fast. Incredibly fast. I wonder what they're eating to get all those calories."

"People," Julie said.

"They're tearing up bodies but not consuming them," Greg said, shaking his head. "I don't think the murders are about feeding.

Maybe they feed if they have time, but if all they wanted were bodies, they'd pick off homeless people, and we wouldn't even know a thing."

"I don't know how smart they are, but even if they're intelligent, they don't know anything about where they are or what's happening. They think we're the enemy. Anyone who gets close enough for them to see—or maybe smell—they have to track down and kill."

"There are a lot of people who work around here and haven't gotten killed," Julie said.

Greg nodded. "That's true. I don't know exactly what an outsider has to do to become a threat. But I think I was getting to something there. What the hell was it?"

"People aren't the outsiders. These things are the outsiders here," she mused. "Outsiders are always scared."

Greg thought about that for a moment. From Pinecotton to L.A. had been a heck of a move. He'd been the outsider.

"Yes," he said. "Let's think about what outsiders do in a strange place."

He'd plunked himself down in an apartment right next to the campus. For the first year, he'd hardly ventured into the surrounding neighborhoods. He'd been fed lurid crime stories by the older students—every freshman was. And there was race. He'd known maybe half a dozen Black kids at his high school. Certainly, he never thought of himself as racist. Toby Williamson was the blackest Black guy he'd ever met, and they'd been best friends his senior year. But he found out in L.A. that he did, indeed, make distinctions. A Black student on campus was different from a couple of Black guys of the same age walking down the street in hoodies. Greg hated revisiting the memory, but he felt it had something to tell him.

"Okay, you're an outsider," he said. "You stay where you feel safe, stay with your own kind. If you have to venture out, or you just feel brave or curious, you make a short trip, then you hurry back. If you have to move—remember, after my first year, they tore that old apartment building down? If you have to move, you try to move just a little bit. Stay nearby, find a place like the place you knew."

Julie gave him a nod. Her voice was a bit soft, comforting. "You moved to the West Campus Apartments. Where you met me."

"Another safe place. Heck, you kept urging me to go out and see some of the neighborhood." When they'd walked out at night, he'd expected to be mugged every minute, but he was a guy, wasn't he? Couldn't show fear in front of a girl.

"And so, what about these outsiders?"

"They'll do the same. Move as little as they have to. Find places that are like living in the dolmen. Try to stay away from strangers—humans. And whatever the trigger is, they kill any people who get too close to finding them."

"And that includes us?"

"Seems so. Not here, though. It's pretty clear they're not active in daylight."

"As far as we know." She opened the car door and perched sideways on the edge of the back seat. "What should we do? Leave town?"

"I don't know. I doubt the cops would let us, anyway. We must be material witnesses or something. You're the attorney. What do you think?"

"You're right. They'd never let us just disappear. If I remember right, the LAPD doesn't really have a budget for protective custody—they'd probably need even more of a direct threat to justify it. Of course, by the time they decide that..."

Greg tried to pull himself together and was a bit surprised when he succeeded.

"Julie, these things aren't super-powered," he said. "They failed to get us at your apartment. They're vicious, but they're also small. There's no reason to think they won't die like anyone else if you shoot them. The only reason they've survived is because no one knew they existed."

"So, what happens now?"

"My guess is that they've got a tunnel dug under that dolmen. If we can find that, they can be dug out and captured or, if necessary, killed."

"What do you mean 'if necessary'?" Julie demanded. "Greg, these things killed Walt!"

"I know. But if they really are some kind of primitive species, it would be hard to kill them for what they think of as protecting themselves."

"Not for me, it wouldn't!" she cried. "But Greg, if they're so different—if they really lay eggs or turn into those tuns or something like that—where could they have come from?"

"I don't know," he said, glad to get off the topic of killing. "Probably tuns were a bad comparison. We don't really know anything about them."

A moment later, Welles came back with a dark-featured cop in an expensively tailored civilian blue suit. The newcomer was introduced as Lieutenant Dave Billings.

"The coroner's here for the body," Welles said. "At first glance, he thinks it was an animal. Mr. Preston, Lieutenant Billings, is our supervisor here at RHD. Please tell him what you told me about your theory."

Surprised at the opening, Greg stood up a little unsteadily. Leaning on the side of the car, he mentioned the evidence so far and sketched his idea of the korrigans.

Billings just stared at him. "Mister, you're so full of it. It's coming out your ears," he scoffed. "Detective Welles, please don't tell me you've actually been listening to this crap."

Welles hesitated. "Sir, I didn't at first. I've already called him crazy. But hell if I know what else fits the facts."

"I do. I don't know what you've been smoking in your off-time, but this guy was either ripped up by a knife or killed by some trained animal. We've got a murder, and we don't need to believe in fairies to explain it. This is your case, Detective, but if I hear any more about this, it won't be." He shook his head, making even more obvious his utter disbelief that a fellow cop would even think about the subject.

They stayed at the scene quite a while until Welles had satisfied himself that all pertinent evidence was collected, and the coroner had driven off with the remains.

As evening approached, the foursome piled back into the car and headed north.

"Billings has to be convinced," Greg said. "Why can't he see what's in front of him?"

Welles turned to face his backseat passenger. "Mr. Preston, you haven't convinced me yet, either. Or even the Counselor here, I'll bet."

"Yes, he has," Julie said. "It sounds as crazy to me as anyone else, but I believe there's something—well, crazy, unexplainable. You tell me what's been tearing up rooms and people by crawling out of little air vents."

Greg smiled. He hadn't expected the support. They clasped hands tightly. *You and me against the world.*

"Maybe we'll have some lab reports when we get back," Fernandez said. "Maybe they'll indicate a normal explanation. Or just maybe, they will prove your case."

Welles stared at his partner. "Gary, I'm a little surprised. I thought I was the one who did wild hunches."

"I'm not convinced yet. But, Alan, you know I was a boy in rural Mexico. Before we immigrated—legally," he added, with a smile into the rearview mirror, "I lived in a town named Ceballos. Next to it is a patch of desert called *la Zona de Silencio.*"

"The Zone of Silence," Greg said. "I've heard of it."

"In the Zone, there are strange lights in the sky at night. The cacti grow red and purple, not green. The land tortoises around our town had no tails and have shells made of triangular segments, where no other turtle in the world—even the same species outside the Zone—has a shell like that. All these strange things in one little area around our town. So I grew up with strangeness, Mr. Preston. I'm far from believing your theory but keeping my mind open at least."

"Thank you for that, at least," Greg said. "Like you say, maybe the lab evidence will tell us something."

They'd just gotten back to headquarters when Welles got a call from the lab. Welles talked briefly and then asked the technician to come over and brief them in person.

"Normally, we don't make them run over here," Welles told Greg.

"But Regional Crime Lab at Cal State's only about ten miles east of here, and this is so weird I want the guy in person. Besides, it's fun to make them go out in the heat like the rest of us."

About half an hour later, an owlish technician turned up, sweating profusely. Welles showed them to a meeting room.

"Okay, Ralph," Welles said. "What've you got?"

"I've got questions not answers," the tech answered in an accent with a trace of New York. "None of the marks on the items you sent in were made with a knife. They do look like claw marks, but the few particles of foreign matter the coroner recovered weren't from metal blades, and they don't look like they're from claws. They are organic, but at first glance, they're more like tooth enamel. We're going to do a mass spec analysis. I know the coroner has one of their top guys, Dr. Sporkin, looking at it, too. Be interesting to see what he thinks."

Welles furrowed his bushy brows. "Ever seen anything like this?"

"Definitely not." He shot a little smile at Greg and Julie. "I've spent my whole career with SID, and these detective types never stop coming up with surprises. We had one guy with a deep forehead wound where the particles recovered turned out to be leather. That screwed us up good until we found out a hooker he tried to rob had nailed him with a spike-heeled shoe."

"Okay, okay," Welles said. "Tell war stories some other time. Is there anything else useful you can tell me?"

"Not yet—not for certain, anyway. Look, Detective, I said 'ok' when you asked me to come over because I thought maybe you'd tell me a little more than you were willing to say on the phone. This obviously isn't your ordinary murder case, and I could help you a lot more if I had a better idea of what you thought I was looking for."

Welles gave him a sympathetic glance but shook his head. "Sorry, Ralph. Can't do that yet. Let us know anything else you find."

Ralph nodded. "Okay. I figured that's how you were playing it. Next, you're going to say this is my top priority from here on out."

"Damn right."

With the technician gone, the others exchanged frustrated

glances. "This is getting worse," Welles growled. "Tooth marks? How could anything get its teeth on the vent like that?"

"It couldn't," Greg said. "Maybe the lab jumped to a conclusion. I'm not a zoologist, but I did own a cat once. I know what a claw mark looks like."

"Well, we've struck out so far with the Lieutenant and SID," Welles said. "What the hell? Let's call the coroner and try for strike three."

The detective phoned the county medical examiner's office. He talked for only a moment before hanging up and turning to the others.

"Well, that examiner Ralph mentioned, Dr. Sporkin? I know the guy. Seems he was about to call me. He's working late tonight because he can't figure out our friend Robert Martin. So we're all going for another ride."

It took only ten minutes to drive to a four-story pile of brick and beige-painted concrete on North Mission Road. It looked like an old hospital or college administration building, with its decorative façade and broad stone front steps. They entered through an innocuously cheery atrium and signed in with the receptionist. As Welles got them visitor badges, Greg noticed a sign with directions to the "Skeletons in the Closet" shop on the second floor.

He nudged Julie. "That sign has got to be someone's idea of a joke."

She smiled. "Not in L.A., it doesn't. I've been in there. It's really a gift shop."

Greg could do nothing but shake his head. *Los Angeles*.

With the formalities taken care of, the receptionist directed the visitors to a small conference room. There, a tall, balding white man wearing a lab coat and thick glasses rose introduced himself as Dr. John Sporkin.

"Hi, doc," Welles said. "We worked on that homicide down on Frat Row, remember?"

"I do. Please, everyone, take a seat." He peered over the top of his glasses at Welles. "Detective, what do you believe killed Mr. Martin?"

"I thought you were supposed to tell me."

Sporkin shook his head. "Not this time, I'm afraid. Detective, I've been here twelve years. I thought I'd seen every possible cause of death."

"And you were wrong," Greg said.

"I was very, very wrong."

12

"How wrong is '"very?"'" Welles asked.

"I'm bewildered," Sporkin replied. "As I told your office this morning, the wounds don't match anything I can find. I had Dr. Kerns from the L.A. Zoo take a look. He couldn't match them, either."

"You said nothing was eaten from the body, right?" Greg asked.

"Correct. It was just savagely ripped up."

"The problem is that, as Dr. Kerns explained, most predatory animals kill with a bite. There are no bite marks on Mr. Martin's body. The only large predator that routinely kills with its forelimbs is the jaguar, and Dr. Kerns was quite definite that the apparent claw marks show the wrong pattern for a jaguar.

"Next, there are claw marks deep in the bones themselves. The claws of most animals aren't hard enough to make those marks without fracturing the bone around them. This animal has claws like steel. Dr. Kearns advised me there are some analogues, like lions and honey badgers, but they're frighteningly sharp.

"Finally, there are some strange puncture wounds in some of the bones. I don't know yet what made them. Under the SEM—our Scanning Electron Microscope—we can see some particles of foreign matter. I think the SID has already told you they couldn't figure those out. All I can say now is that the bone wounds were made by something with a larger diameter and a straighter tip than the claws."

"Could these be our missing tooth marks?" Greg asked.

Sporkin shrugged. "I don't know. It would be odd just to crack some holes in the major bones and not leave any other tooth marks, but it's as good a guess as any. Perhaps if it had really long incisors. We're still doing the autopsy on Thomas Windsor, but so far, it looks very similar.

"Finally, there's blood missing. There was a lot of blood around Mr. Martin's body, but there was hardly any left in it, and the amounts don't add up. I have no idea why that is. That's why I'm asking you what killed these men."

Welles shifted uneasily. "Is this just between us? Off the record?"

Sporkin nodded. "If you like."

"Mr. Preston, here, is sort of an expert on weird phenomena."

Sporkin smiled. "I thought I recognized the name. I read your novel about what would happen if we captured a real sasquatch. Very well researched."

"Thank you."

"Anyway," Welles went on, "Greg has a theory"—he paused— "an idea that maybe these deaths were caused by some sort of apelike animal—like an ape dwarf. He thinks it came over from England with the tomb Mr. Windsor imported."

"I see," Sporkin said. "You'll forgive me for being, shall I say, extremely skeptical."

"I will," Greg said, nodding. "But speculate. A short, very strong creature. Think of a murderous orangutan with clawed hands. Could that have made the wounds?"

"If—IF—there was any such thing, I suppose it could have," Sporkin said. "But I'm not about to put that on a death certificate. The fact I haven't found a more mundane explanation doesn't mean there isn't one."

"'There are more things in heaven and earth...'"

Welles ignored him and replied to Sporkin. "Agreed, doc. Please keep looking into it. Do everything you know how to do."

"Believe me, we will. I've already heard there's political interest in this case. Our two decedents were very different men, but both seem to have had friends in high places. We have Mr. Windsor down in Room B now—what we call our VIP room. We'll keep working until we find something."

* * *

It was dark when they left the building.

"What now?" Julie asked.

"I talked to the lieutenant earlier about some kind of protective arrangement—maybe even parking you in the jail for a while if we couldn't find anything else," Welles said. "He won't buy it."

"Why not?"

"Paperwork. I work for a guy who likes being a boss so much that he's forgotten that being a cop comes first. He's not a dummy, but he doesn't get a lot of respect in RHD. 'Course, maybe he'd say the same thing about me. Anyway, even though you two are the closest thing to witnesses on a multiple homicide, he says he doesn't see the need. And putting a detail to watch you at your hotel would be even more paperwork, plus manpower he doesn't have."

"Just great," Julie said, narrowing her eyes.

Welles glanced at Greg. "How's that hotel you're in for security?"

"Pretty good," Greg said. "All the air vents are small. The outside walls are sheer glass, and the door and the deadbolt lock looked pretty solid."

"Sounds safe enough. Look, I'll put the word out to the next patrol shift to drive by and keep an eye out. If you think anything funny's going on, yell for help."

They reached Welles' car, and the detective handed Greg a card. "If I'm not in and you need me, that has my home number. My wife wishes I wouldn't give it out so much, but sometimes you have to. And there's one other thing."

He fished out his keys and opened the trunk of the Accord. "Preston, you know how to use a shotgun?"

Greg gave him a surprised look. "As a kid hunting rabbits, and I've done some skeet shooting. I have a friend in Sacramento who's a fanatic, so I go with him sometimes."

"Pump-action?"

"Yes. Twelve-gauge."

"Good." He handed Greg a leather gun bag. "The L-T would kill me if he knew I loaned a gun to a civilian—even though it's my gun and not the department's. But my gut feeling is you two might need it."

Greg took the gun. Despite his having handled such a weapon before, it felt heavy and strange in his hands. "Thanks for the concern," he said uneasily.

"I'd give you something smaller, but with this, your aim doesn't have to be so good. I'm taking a big chance here that you're not the type who's gonna panic and blow holes in the door."

"You can trust him," Julie said firmly.

Welles nodded. He reached into the trunk again and pulled out a golf bag. "Slide it in here," he said. "Let's not have the bellhop going nuts."

"Thanks," Greg said.

* * *

Greg and Julie returned to their room without incident. With the door secured, Greg pulled out the shotgun. It was a Remington 12-gauge pump, a bit worn but well cared for. "Ever fire one of these?" he asked.

"No. My parents hated guns. All guns. There were times as a lawyer I've wanted one, but I've never learned to shoot."

"I hope you don't have to shoot this time, either. But if you need to, it could be what keeps you alive. It's really not hard to handle."

"That's our new reality, isn't it?" she said.

"I'm afraid so."

"Would this stop them?"

"It should. It doesn't matter how strong our three-or four-foot dwarf is. It's a physics thing. The impact will still flatten it."

After they spent enough time reviewing the gun's operation to make Julie comfortable, Greg slid the gun under the edge of the bed. "It'll be right here," he said. "Rule One is never to leave a gun ready to shoot, but if we need this, we won't have any time to fumble iaround."

Julie bit her lower lip. "Do you think they'll find us?"

"I don't know. I don't know how they tracked Walt. They couldn't have followed him in broad daylight. It must have been by scent." His eyebrows went up at a sudden thought. "We ought to get some pepper spray. If these things can smell like that, they need noses like wolves or bloodhounds. Pepper spray should be almost as nasty as buckshot to them."

"Allow me," Julie said. She pulled a white plastic canister out of her handbag. "Never without it in this town."

"Okay, good. Even if they're tracking by scent, we don't know how good they are. I've got no idea how long it would take them to follow us over a distance like this. Our using a cab should help: it wouldn't smell like your car. Just to be safe—wait, that's it!"

"What's what?"

"That spot on your car tire. Korrigan urine or saliva or something. They don't know what a car is, but they know there's this thing you move in, so they marked it. Pretty damn smart of them."

"Scary smart," Julie said. "In case you're right, we'd better stop using the car. What else were you saying?"

"That I suppose we ought to move every couple of nights until— well, whenever."

"We don't know very damn much, do we, Greg?" she asked. "God, look at me. When you knew me in school, I was always the focused one. Go, go, go, study, study, work, work. Now I feel like I'm a helpless wreck."

"Julie, if this wasn't incredibly upsetting to you, you'd have to be insane," Greg said. He sat next to her on the bed and put his arm around her, instantly aware of how fast her heart was beating. He felt like falling apart too but convinced himself it wasn't an option.

He turned his attention to Julie. She was clenching her fists on her knees.

"I am not going to let this get me," she insisted. "I am *not* surrendering here." She looked up at Greg and forced a little smile. "Well, if we're going to war, I guess we'd better keep our strength up, huh? Let's try to eat something."

They ordered from room service and settled down in front of the TV. Julie tried all the cable news channels, but Windsor didn't seem to be national news yet, and mentions of Martin were just recycled. The news online wasn't much more informative. Social media, of course, was a different story. There were already thousands of posts declaring Martin was murdered by racists who supported the museum, by the LAPD, or by the Deep State.

When the late local news came on, Tom Windsor's murder was the lead story. "Mr. Windsor, an eccentric and controversial figure, was discovered in a shallow grave on the grounds of his own museum," intoned Delvecchio.

"Spokesmen for the police department, which has been notably uncooperative during this and other recent homicides, declined to speculate on whether this killing was related to the recent protests against the museum or to the unsolved murder of protest leader Robert Martin. Even the details of Mr. Windsor's fatal injury are being withheld."

"I'll bet that won't change anytime soon," Greg said.

"This is the third death in two weeks that may be related to the museum," Delvecchio continued. "The first was that of writer Walter Rivas, whose body was found in his apartment on the eighteenth."

The show continued with a brief shot of Windsor's body being wheeled away. Then Karen Montrose came on and did a standup on front of the gate to Windsor's estate, sketching the museum's history.

"The police have ordered the museum shut down and the grounds cordoned off," she said. "A spokesman refused to elaborate on the reasons beyond saying the officers wanted to search for more evidence. One officer, however, told me there's a possibility the killer is still hiding somewhere on the estate grounds. We'll follow developments in this bizarre case very closely and bring you any new information as soon as it's available. This is Karen Montrose, Live News, near Griffith Park."

As they had done the night before, they checked the other local channels, then cycled through CNN, MSNBC, and their brethren one more time. No luck.

Greg got up and turned off the set. "Well, what do you make of that?"

"They might just be looking for evidence, but I think that anonymous comment is closer to the mark," Julie said. "If they keep the estate sealed off, it just might mean they're starting to believe you."

"They don't believe me," Greg said. "They just don't know what the hell to do."

13

Vladimir "Pete" Petrovsky locked the front door of Pete's Wholesale Meats and grinned at his thirteen-year-old son. "That's it, Sergei. A good day!"

"Since that idiot man from the catering service finally paid up?"

Pete laughed. "Yes, exactly!" He had to admit Sergei was his favorite son. Polite, not like his brother. Nikolai couldn't make a sentence without swearing and cared little about anything but his computer games. Petrovsky knew people made good careers out of computers and software, and he hoped Nikolai would come out all right, but his lessons about respect and hard work had taken root easily with Sergei. With Nikolai, it was a fight.

"And you finished the receipts?" he asked Sergei.

"Yes, Father. Someone overpaid by two dollars."

"Ah ha, we're rich!"

The thud echoed from the freezer room, seeming to shake the entire concrete building.

"Father, what's that?"

The second thud came, then lesser but more frightening sounds —tearing and cracking.

"Father, is this what Tony Hardy talked about?"

Petrovsky froze. They'd all talked about it five months ago. A meatpacker's business broken into through the ceiling, Jack Hardy killed by some crazy knife-wielding intruder, his six-year-old son left screaming incoherently. Meat stolen, almost a hundred pounds of it. The police never found anything.

Petrovsky motioned sharply to the office closet. "Hide in there! Go!"

Sergei did as he was told.

Petrovsky tossed him his cell phone. "Call the police! The nine-one-one! Now!"

"What will you do?"

Petrovsky raised a cleaver. "No one will touch you, I promise. Any crazy man in here will be a dead man!"

Sergei leaped into the closet as his father raised a cleaver.

Petrovsky opened the door and stepped into the long room where the sides of beef hung. When he was a child and his father the butcher, he had prowled among these slabs, pretending they were the big predatory dinosaurs in the movies and he the determined caveman trying to ambush and spear the great beasts.

He could tell the room was too warm, and the outside air was coming through the ceiling. He could see stars if he looked right. Where the roof had been broken through was a great pool of shadow from which he could hear the sound of breaking ribs.

"Who's there? *Svoloch!* Get out!" he yelled.

The attack came from the side, taking him down hard as something stabbed deep into his left shoulder. He screamed and half-rolled and chopped with the cleaver, a short stroke but one empowered by thirty years of hard work and all the adrenalin in his body. The cleaver bit deep, and Petrovsky was free. He was halfway to his feet when he heard someone else behind him, and the world vanished into a kaleidoscope of color and pain.

One minute later, as Sergei was still yelling into his phone at the operator, who couldn't understand what was happening, the closet door exploded inward.

14

D anger. *The Clan is in danger.*
  There were too many Tall Ones around the Home Place. The male and female, with the scent of curiosity and suspicion about them, had been twice near the Home Place. Since the reckless one had killed the old Tall One and left his body right next to the Home Place, everything was worse. They would have to run. Run where?

They could use the Stinking Holes to conceal their movements but could not stay, could not make a Home Place there...Terrible smells and vapors and strange liquids overwhelmed smell, stung the eyes, brought dizziness. Can't stay in the Holes.

There had to be a new Home Place. But first, the Curious Ones had to be killed. They could not live.

Half the Clan gathered in shadow near the great glass hill where the scent told them the Curious Ones were hiding. The hill was hollow, but there were far too many Tall Ones inside to just go in. Two of the most dexterous members of the Clan began the long, dangerous climb.

15

―――――――

"We'd better get some rest," Julie said.

"Let's do one more check." Greg went to the door and verified the doorknob lock, deadbolt, and chain were all set. He'd done this at least twice since room service had come and gone.

Julie perched on the bed in her sleepshirt, watching his every move.

"I'll keep the gun ready on my side," he said. "If you hear anything, and I'm asleep, wake me up, no matter how unsure you are. We can't take any chances."

She nodded. "Have you ever been this scared?"

"Not even close."

"Me, neither." She paused. "I want to thank you."

"For what?"

"For being here. You didn't have to come. And I...I don't have any right to ask you to risk your life. What I'm trying to say is...I mean this. You can leave if you want."

"No, I can't," he said. He studied her face. It had taken real guts for her to say that, even if she'd assumed and hoped he'd turn down the offer.

"I don't know what the hell's happening," he said. "This korrigan idea still seems so totally ridiculous. But something or someone killed Walt. He was my friend, which makes this my business. That may sound like a speech from a bad movie, but I mean it. I'm not a hero, whatever that is, but maybe I am, just by luck, the guy who can help here."

He looked closely at her face again, their eyes meeting. "And finally, there's no way in hell I'll leave you to face a time like this alone."

Then their faces were floating closer, their hands finding each other. They kissed, hard. Then their bodies came together, with the frantic passion of people not so concerned with what they were doing as with simple escape from the rest of the world.

Neither one of them spoke or even thought as they tore off their clothes and tumbled down onto the bed. Neither one wanted to think.

After the lovemaking, they held each other tightly, focused on the closeness, warmth, and comfort of being together. In a semi-conscious movement, Greg turned out the bedside lamp and pulled a blanket over them. After a very few minutes, they both slipped into an exhausted, grateful sleep.

Some indeterminable time later, one of them moved. They both slowly rose to a state closer to waking. Aware more than ever of the warmth of Julie's body against his, he pulled her closer. She responded. Without saying a word, they began to make love again. This time, it was slow, gentle, and caring, as they caressed each other for long minutes. It was a giving and receiving of strength, but Greg felt something else, too. He felt like he had never met her before and yet was drawn to her with a force he'd never felt. As he explored her body, once familiar but now somehow new, he was consciously trying to draw everything out. He wanted to give her comfort and pleasure for as long as possible.

When it was finally over, and he was recovering his breath, Greg tried to hold on to those feelings. He couldn't. Thoughts of comfort and pleasure slithered almost instantly out of Greg's mind, replaced by something hard and cold.

What the hell are you doing?

Suddenly flooded with guilt and uncertainty, Greg drew back from Julie. She opened her eyes to look for him and half-saw him through the darkness. He was sitting on the edge of the bed, clenching and unclenching his hands, looking as if he was in pain.

"Greg, what is it?"

"What is it?" he asked in a voice full of confusion. "What it is is that the guy I called my best friend hasn't been dead for two weeks, and I just had sex with his fiancée. That's what's wrong, damn it!"

He could feel Julie's glare even in the darkness. "Thank you for referring to me like I'm an inanimate object! I do have feelings of my own, you know, and now that you've brought it up, they're making me feel like shit, thank you!"

"I'm sorry. I'm sorry. I didn't mean it to sound that way. I just feel like a total jerk right now."

She grabbed his wrist and pulled him around to face her. "Damn it, think for a minute. In the first place, I'm not a tramp who sleeps around whenever she feels like it. There are feelings between us, Greg. I loved Walt—and somehow, for some screwed-up reason, I still love you, too."

She didn't give him time to react to that. "And in the second place, we may both be murdered at any time by some kind of monsters that can't possibly exist. Nobody—not Walt, not God Himself—is going to blame us for grabbing for comfort wherever we find it."

He managed a thin smile. "I just meant—" he broke off, raising a hand for silence.

"What is it?" she whispered.

"Door." As quietly as he could, he rolled off the bed and fumbled for the shotgun. They could hear it now—quick, light footsteps in the hall. Greg brought the shotgun up and pumped it.

"Get behind the bed," he whispered. She clambered off the bed but instead crouched next to him as he trained the gun on the door.

The footsteps went past the door, began to fade, then turned back. A shadow broke the crack of light under the door, and Greg felt his hands grow slick as he gripped the shotgun. He strained to see in the darkness as he waited for the door to burst in.

"Timmy, get back here! Do you know how late it is?"

"Yes, Mommy."

The footsteps scurried off down the hallway.

Greg and Julie collapsed on the bed, laughing in hysterical relief.

"I can't take another episode like that," Greg gasped.

"I can't either," Julie giggled, wiping her eyes. "Maybe we needed —Greg!"

The terror in her voice made him snap his head around to follow her pointing arm. Through the window curtains, the dim light outside showed the vague silhouette of a moving figure's top half.

"The curtains," Greg whispered harshly as his heart pounded on his ribs. He scuttled to his left, raising the gun toward the window. "Julie, pull the damn curtains!"

Physically shaking off her paralysis, Julie reached up, grabbed the curtain cord, and yanked hard. Almost in the same motion, she dove across the bed, scrambling away from the window as the curtain was jerked open.

Greg stared at the nightmare.

He couldn't make out the face through the window, just the outline of a child-sized head and the malevolent glare of two large deep-set eyes glinting like black diamonds.

Greg flung himself backward as the window crashed in.

His back thumped against a dresser as the thing climbed inside, and he distantly heard Julie scream as his hands moved of their own volition.

The boom of the shotgun deafened him. For an instant, the room was lit, and in that flash, he saw the korrigan hurled back through the window, arms flailing for purchase.

And then it was gone.

Greg dropped the gun. He and Julie groped toward each other in the dark, touched, and held each other tightly.

"Oh, God," she breathed, trembling. "Oh, God."

Greg trembled, too, but he couldn't find any words.

Outside the door came the sound of heavy footsteps running. Then a fist hammered on the door.

"Open up! Hotel security!"

"Call the police!" Greg shouted. "Detective Alan Welles, Robbery-Homicide! You hear me? Alan Welles!"

* * *

Greg and Julie found the presence of mind to throw on some clothes. Greg cautiously kept the shotgun pointed toward the window, but there was no sight or sound of further intrusion. Apparently discomfited by the gunshot, the hotel staff made no effort to open the door until the police arrived to take over.

"This is Welles!" The authoritative tone sounded familiar now. "Open up."

Greg put down the shotgun and opened the door. Welles and Fernandez stepped inside.

"Holy shit," Welles said, surveying the damage. "What the hell did you shoot at?"

"A myth."

Welles glared at him. "You weren't dreaming, by any chance, were you? Or got a little edgy, just thought you saw something in the eighth-floor window?"

Greg sank on the bed next to Julie. "Look at the glass, Detective," he said. "A lot of it's broken in, not out."

Welles edged toward the window. It was after six AM now, and the light outside was growing. The detective peered at the shattered glass, aluminum framing, and wallboard surrounding the hole.

"There's blood on the edge here," he said, gesturing at a shard of glass that still clung in its place. "Blood or something like it."

"We blew the korrigan out the window," Greg said. "The body's got to be down on the sidewalk."

"We didn't notice one," Welles said. He turned to his partner. "Gary, take some uniforms down and secure the area. Maybe it fell behind a car or something."

"Right." Fernandez vanished into the crowd of police and hotel staff gathered around the doorway.

"Simmonds?" Welles called.

A young patrolman appeared. "Yes, sir?"

"This room gets sealed off. Nobody, including hotel staff, gets in. Make sure someone stays at the door till I call back." Welles turned back to Greg and Julie. "You two. I want you downtown right now."

Greg looked at the room one more time. "Pretty soon, we're not going to be able to rent anywhere in this city." The joke fell flat.

Thirty minutes later, they were in the now-familiar confines of the conference room. Welles sat them down and proffered styrofoam cups of coffee. Despite not being regular coffee drinkers, both accepted. Greg remembered the way he'd thought of Julie's tea as something nice and normal.

"All right," Welles said. "Whole story, beginning to end."

They told the tale in fits and starts, interrupting each other, forgetting details, and then going back to recount them. Often, they found themselves grasping hands for support.

When they had finished, Welles shook his head. "What the hell am I going to do with a story like this?"

"Alan, we're telling the truth," Julie said.

"I believe you're telling what happened the way you remember it," Welles said. "Problem: my lieutenant or anyone else is still going to think you're crazy."

"I don't see where you have a choice," Greg said. "Take our statements straight, give them to your boss, and whatever happens, happens. He can't blame you if he thinks we're psychos. Me, I'm too busy being glad I'm alive to care what anyone thinks of me."

Welles thought for a moment. "Wait here for a bit. I need to make some calls. You two want some doughnuts or something?"

"I think so," Greg said.

"Somebody always brings a box in from BabyCakes or Spudnuts. We take turns."

"Stereotype city," Greg said when Welles had gone.

Julie shot him a grin. "What's the stereotype? That cops always have doughnuts, or you can always eat no matter what's happening?"

Greg shrugged. "Both?"

* * *

When Welles returned, he closed the door and slumped into a chair, wearing a grim expression.

"Well, I've got some news. First, I jawed with the hotel. They won't press any charges if you pay for damages."

"Press charges? For what?" Greg demanded.

"Think about it, Genius. You smuggled in a gun and blew up their room. You wanna try to sell them your dwarf story?"

Julie put a restraining hand on Greg's arm. "Believe me, they could think of a dozen things to have us charged with. Paying damages is the easy way out. Thank you, Alan."

"You're welcome. Second piece of news: there is no body under your window."

Greg's eyes widened. "That's impossible. The damn thing fell eight floors!"

"There's a cracked square on the sidewalk. Something like blood on it. We took pieces for analysis. That's it."

"The others took it away," Greg suggested. "There had to be others."

"Maybe. Question: how did it, or they, or whatever, get to the eighth floor in the first place?'

"There must be a way," Greg said. "Don't buildings like that have tracks for window-washing platforms?"

"They do, but no one could climb them—not without equipment. They design them that way."

"It might be a different story if you had claws," Greg said.

"Well, we know you had an intruder of some kind. We've got bloodstains, plus some kind of tissue off that window. We sent it all to our buddy Ralph at SID, and he'll coordinate with Sporkin at the coroner. We want all the brains we've got on this."

"Now for the fun part. I didn't go to the L-T. I went to Captain Lear. He's commander of Robbery-Homicide. Billings'll chew my ass, but tough. I never saw a case like this, and Billings won't know how to handle it. There'll be all kinds of political flack 'cause of Martin. He's what we call a high-jingo case all by himself. But we have to fend that off and get back to solving these murders."

Greg knew bureaucracy—any bureaucracy—well enough to know Welles' action would cost him. "We appreciate what you're doing," he said.

"Like you said, I don't seem to have much choice, but thanks anyway. I want to get a conference on this with Lear and Sporkin. Lear said okay—we'll go for one o'clock if Sporkin thinks he's got enough for us by then.

"Before we get to that, though, I want to know something. If these things exist, why are they killing people? Why don't they just run for the hills and hide?"

"You're still saying 'if,'" Greg noted.

"Yeah. Not because I think you're lying. Because if I admit to myself there are homicidal dwarves from the days of King Arthur running around Los Angeles, they won't have to throw me in the loony bin because I'll sign myself in."

"Fair enough. Well, I don't know why no one else on the museum staff has been killed. It might be what Windsor mentioned—that they don't go near the dolmen. These things are scared. The dolmen is the only familiar thing to them. They'll stay near it as long as they can.

"As to the killings, my best guess if that a lot of what's happened is sheer chance—whoever's digging around the dolmen when the korrigans are out, or whoever they get a good sight or a smell of, gets killed. I wonder if Martin ever trespassed onto the estate."

Welles looked at him, a little surprised. "Good guess. We arrested him for coming on the grounds at night once, along with a guy with a video camera. They actually climbed up on top of that dolmen. Out on bail the next day."

"He's lucky he didn't die right then," Greg said. "We don't know how these things think, but that face I saw—well, if something that inhuman could have an expression, it was hate."

"That's my last question. You say you got a look at its face. How good a look?"

"It was good." A quick shudder ran through Greg's body as he forced the memory up. "I can't forget it if I wanted to. I just close my eyes, and it's like seeing a photograph."

"Good. Because I've got a sketch artist waiting outside. If these things are real, I at least want to know what they look like."

"No, you don't," Greg said. "Believe me. But I'll try."

* * *

When the sketch was finished, the quick-fingered artist held it up, his multiple earrings jangling. The two witnesses took a look.

'That's it." Greg said. His stomach tightened, and he turned away. "It's a lot worse in person, but that's it."

"Counselor?"

Julie nodded. "I didn't get as good a look, but that sure as hell looks like it to me."

Welles studied the picture for a moment. "That's the ugliest thing I've ever seen. We'll see how it impresses the captain later." He turned to the artist. "Ken, until you hear something different from Captain Lear or me, you never drew this. Understood?"

The artist shrugged. "Whatever."

The detective turned to the witnesses. "This case is so screwy we forgot our own procedures. We should have started with separate taped statements in the interview rooms. Let's get that done."

"Anyplace with no monsters is good to me," Julie said.

* * *

They made their statements. Sporkin called twice to postpone the conference, saying he was still testing the evidence. Someone took a sandwich order from a place called Philippe's. The detectives made calls and computer searches on this case and others, once venturing out to interrogate an unrelated witness, while Greg and Julie parked in an empty cubicle next to the detectives and talked about anything except the murders.

It was after four when the two detectives got news.

"You'll like this," Welles said in a voice Greg couldn't read.

"What's happening?" Julie asked.

"I asked one of our other teams to take another look at your apartment building. I wanted to know if an intruder really got into the air vents and how he got in."

"What do they find?"

"The air conditioning plant is down on the floor with the parking garage. In the main duct running into the building, someone had pried a piece of loose sheet metal off. They'd bent it back, but you could still see where the screws were popped out. Made a hole about two feet square." He hesitated a moment. "I was an idiot for not thinking to look. I'm sorry. It might have gotten people believing you quicker."

"Alan, no harm done," Julie said. "It wouldn't have changed anything."

"Thanks. It's also time to go for a ride."

They were met on the steps of the coroner's building by Captain Patrick Lear, a slender, silver-haired man with a thin face aged by the concerns of his position. As introductions were made, Greg noted how carefully Lear listened to them and watched their faces, trying to size them up for himself. Lieutenant Billings came out of the building to meet them. He gave Welles an incendiary glare but limited his speech to a stiffly formal greeting to his captain.

Sporkin was waiting in the conference room. He wore blue papery-looking scrubs and smelled of chemicals Greg couldn't identify. With him, dressed in a khaki shirt and pants, was a portly, bearded man whom he introduced as Dr. Philip Kerns from the zoo.

"I've asked Dr. Kerns to be here because some of our findings seem to fall more into his area of expertise than mine," Sporkin said. "I hope you don't mind."

"If he can help, he's welcome," Lear said. "Detective Welles, close the door, please."

Welles did, and Lear motioned everybody to sit around the laminated-wood ochre tabletop.

"All right, let's get started," Lear said. "To put it as simply as possible, we're here to figure out what the hell's going on. As a reminder to any writers present, this is so far off the record that none of us were ever here." He gave Greg a stern look. Greg nodded.

"The first rule in finding the truth is admitting what you don't know," Lear continued. "In this case, there's an awful lot of that. What I've heard so far sounds completely unbelievable, but I'm trying not to be closed-minded. Detective Welles, why don't you start by reviewing the Rivas murder."

Welles outlined the facts of the case. He rushed through a couple of places, giving Julie a sympathetic glance. He went on to detail Martin's murder, then the finding of Windsor's body. "Lieutenant, I should let you finish here. What else has come up in the investigation out there?"

"Not a damn thing on Windsor," Billings said. "While you've been listening to Stephen King here, everyone connected with the museum has been questioned. We found a scuffed-up area with some blood that was probably where the killing took place, but that's it."

"There is something else, though," the lieutenant said. "On the Martin killing."

"What's new there?" Lear asked.

"It's gotten more complicated. We can't find the chief witness."

"McGraw?" Welles asked.

Billings nodded. Addressing Lear, he went on, "Captain, McGraw went home that night after we were done and had his statement."

"Steinberg and Russo from RHD took that," Welles said. "Lieutenant, what are you sitting on?"

"According to his wife, McGraw never got home. He drove to his apartment building on Vermont. His car is in the parking lot. But he never turned up at his door."

"Why the hell haven't we heard about this until now?" Welles asked.

"A little respect, please, Detective," Billings said. Turning back to Lear, he said, "It got taken as a routine missing person. Someone remembered the news and called RHD about him just a couple of hours ago. I just sent Russo down for a look."

"Wait a minute," Greg said. "Alan, you said once that Martin and another man had been arrested trespassing into the museum grounds at night. Was that other man—?"

"McGraw," Welles said. "Damn it."

Everyone was silent for a long moment.

Lear spoke up. "Obviously, we need to consider McGraw's disappearance part of this case and investigate it fully. Let's continue here while we wait to see what Russo and Steinberg find on that. Detective Welles?"

Welles finished by recounting the incident in Greg and Julie's hotel room. Then he turned to Greg.

"You're on, Genius," he said. "Let's have the theory."

Greg noted that the ridicule formerly evident when Welles used the "Genius" nickname was no longer quite so obvious. He took that as encouragement. So, with a nod to Welles, he stood up and said what he thought. He began with the legends and supposed historical records of the korrigans. There were startled looks from those who hadn't heard the theory, and Billings shook his head fiercely, but no one interrupted Greg's explanation.

"This morning, I had a look at one close-up," Greg said. "I wish I hadn't. Detective Welles has the police sketch. It's accurate."

Welles held up the sketch.

The creature depicted had a head and two eyes. All resemblance to a human being ended there.

The round, prominent black eyes were set deep in a dark face fringed with spiky dark hair. Below them, the face was all straight lines and angles. There was no obvious nose or mouth. A short, wide beak-like structure projected out from under an indentation that had no immediately obvious purpose.

"Sure as hell is ugly," Billings said. "Like something you'd see on drugs—or so I've heard. You two don't indulge a little, do you?"

Greg started to retort, but Julie squeezed his hand. "Lieutenant, we can understand your skepticism," she said. "Please, consider all the evidence before you decide we're crazy."

"All right, but it won't be easy. I'm not chasing ghosts. I'm after a murderer."

"We want you to catch one," Greg said. "Because we're going to be the next victims if you don't."

"Let's hear your evidence," Lear said, looking at the sketch.

"Well, let's go with the bodies first," Welles said. "Doctor Sporkin?"

Sporkin repeated his description of the wounds. "As I told you earlier, I can't account for the wounds. That's why I brought Dr. Kerns in. Phil, would you tell them what you think?"

"No known animal makes marks quite like that," Kerns said in a quiet, academic tone that belied his bearlike visage. "And none tears up a body like that without eating anything. The paw, or whatever you call it, looks a little like this." He fished a folded piece of paper from his shirt pocket. "I'm no artist, but this might give you an idea."

They passed the drawing around. It showed a hand-like paw with four stubby fingers. One finger was opposed like a thumb, although not as distinctly as on a human. A sharp-looking, slightly hooked claw protruded from each digit.

"I didn't see the hands that clearly, but this looks about right," Greg said.

"It would be consistent with the wounds I've observed," Sporkin added.

"Wicked-looking thing," Welles observed. "How big is it?"

"About six inches across the claw tips," Kerns said. "Smaller than a human hand, but you've seen how effective it is."

Lear licked his lips and reached for a coffee mug. "This is getting very weird," he observed.

Sporkin gave him a grim smile. "Then hold on to your seat, Captain. It's about to get a lot worse."

16

"How much weirder can this get?" Billings snapped. He looked at Lear with a why-the-hell-are-we-here expression.

"You'll see, Lieutenant," Sporkin replied calmly. "If I may continue?"

Lear nodded, and Sporkin went on. "So far, we've been talking about the claw wounds. As I said yesterday, there are other wounds I couldn't explain—punctures in the bones themselves.

"Now it's my turn to pass a picture around." He picked up a large manila envelope and pulled out two color photographs. "These are close-ups of two of the wounds. The first is from Mr. Martin's right iliac crest—the top of the femur," he explained, pointing to his hip. "The second is from Mr. Windsor's sternum or breastbone.

"What these show is a neat round hole. It's not surgical-quality work—there is some cracking around the holes—but otherwise, it looks quite similar to what you see when a trochanter is inserted to remove bone marrow. It's a larger hole than you'd see for a trochanter, but it's done in just the right places to get the maximum amount of marrow.

"There are wounds like these in both iliac crests, the pelvis, the sternum, and several of the long bones of both bodies. The marrow has been drawn out."

"You're right, Doctor, it is getting worse," Lear said. "What made these wounds? Have you seen them before?"

"No," Sporkin replied.

"Some animals do eat bone marrow," Kerns said. "It's a fairly important part of a hyena's diet. The hyena waits until lions have finished with the kill—which they may have stolen from the hyenas in the first place—then cracks open the bones with its stronger jaws. But nothing we know of in nature is purely a marrow-eater. To me, that seems too specialized to be practical."

"As I told Detective Welles, we can't account for all the blood in the last two bodies, either," Sporkin said. "A lot was splashed around in Mr. Martin's case. But in both, there's definitely blood loss."

"Shit, now it's vampires," Billings said in a weary tone. "What next, the abominable snowman?"

"Blood and bone marrow have many of the same components," Sporkin said. "It would make sense for an animal which consumed one to have a taste for the other."

"There's no visible structure on that face you've sketched that would make these bone wounds," Kerns put in. "To toss out a really wild thought, though, maybe what looks like a beak isn't a beak. Maybe it's a cover for some modified proboscis that can penetrate bone." He looked at the sketch again. "I don't really see a nose. This thing must have an entirely different system of smelling than known animals."

Kerns shook his head. "Whatever this thing is, I'd love to get one in the lab—not to mention having one on exhibit. It would sure as hell outdraw the Koala House."

Lear spoke up, waving his hands as if trying to dispel his incredulity. "Let's focus on that. Just suppose we grant that there is some totally unknown animal loose in Los Angeles. What exactly is it?"

"We have some clues regarding its makeup," Sporkin said. "First, from the wounds. The marks of the claws and the puncture wounds reveal particles vaguely resembling tooth enamel, but it doesn't look like it under the microscope. I think we'll pass it to a forensic odontology consultant to be sure.

"SID's Serology/DNA unit has given us some results on the blood. The blood found in the hotel room and on the sidewalk this morning isn't human *or* a known type of animal. There are red cells that resemble ours—it has iron-based hemoglobin—and there's kind of plasma. There are also other components—specifically, two types of cells—that I can't guess the function of. The hemoglobin isn't structured the way it is in any normal vertebrates. There's DNA, but the lab's DQ Alpha test comes back so bizarre I can't draw any conclusions except the creature isn't related to anything else known on this planet."

Greg listened, feeling a little disoriented as the evidence piled up on just how strange and unbelievable these things were. He had seen them, and even he was beginning to feel once again that, somehow, this all couldn't be real.

"Now for the worst part," Sporkin said. "That tissue we got from the hotel. We recovered about twenty grams of material torn off by the shotgun blast. That tissue is what stumps me the most."

He paused for a moment, a bit theatrically. He was obviously waiting for someone to ask why, so Greg did.

"Because we've never seen anything like it in any animal. It appears to be muscle tissue, but it's made up of two kinds of fibers mixed together. One is definitely muscle: there are cells structured a lot like ours, enough to be assignable as vertebrate. The other is the weird stuff.

"It resembles cartilage, but only partly. To give a quick anatomy lesson, you have three kinds of cartilage in your body. Hyaline cartilage is the most common kind. Then you have fibrous cartilage, which is very strong and makes up the disks between the vertebrae, and elastic, which is the most flexible and forms structures like your ears.

"The tissue from the hotel has the flexibility of elastic cartilage and a structure and strength more like fibrous. In other ways, it isn't like either one. Cartilage has no nerves or blood vessels. The sample has both. The cartilage cells themselves are striated—elongated and bundled like the more recognizable muscle fibers."

Greg thought Sporkin seemed incredibly calm describing something so bizarre the paper he'd undoubtedly write on it would put him in contention for a Nobel Prize. Maybe he was practicing for his acceptance speech.

Greg took a guess at where the Sporkin was headed. "Are you saying this thing has muscles that are partly like our muscle and partly like cartilage?"

Sporkin paused, again seemingly for effect. "Incredible as it seems, yes. The ratio of muscle to this quasi-cartilage is about eighty-twenty. I'm generalizing from a small sample, of course, but this animal's muscles are very different from ours. The recognizable muscle fibers are more like our fast-twitch than slow-twitch fibers, with the other kind mixed throughout. If all its muscles are like that, it's not built for endurance but would be a great leaper and extremely strong, not to mention tough."

Welles shook his head. "We started with a short murderer," he mused. "Now you're saying we've got something more like an alien—or maybe like a gargoyle."

"I've noticed the resemblance to gargoyles," Greg said. "It's probably not a coincidence."

"I haven't heard anybody with a plan," Julie said. "As impossible as it seems, some kind of bizarre animal is running around out there. How do we wipe it out?"

"I haven't been convinced they are out there," Billings said in a voice that betrayed his struggle to control sarcasm. "Doctor, even assuming all your analysis is right, that doesn't mean your speculation is. Until we have absolute proof no humans were involved, it's still a homicide investigation."

"Agreed," Lear said. "We'll go full-court with the investigation, and we'll keep in mind that something really weird may be involved.

But we can't panic yet over an unproven—"

Greg slammed his hand down. "Dammit, I saw one of these! We have physical evidence of them! Yes, according to everything we know, they're impossible. But they're here!"

"You saw someone or something in the dark," Billings said.

"In other words, I'm wrong. So where did we get the blood, Lieutenant? How did we fake the tissue?"

"Everyone! Here's how we're going to do this," Lear said, raising his voice. "I agree something very strange is happening. But I think the techniques of a police investigation still apply. We'll proceed with that investigation with an open mind and try to collect more evidence to determine precisely what we're dealing with."

"We have enough evidence," Greg said.

"I don't agree."

"We could go to the press. I'm not the first person to notice the PAB is across the street from the *Times*."

Lear shook his head. "Think about it, Mr. Preston. They'd laugh in your face.

"Now, hold on," he added as Greg started to speak again. "I said I'd keep my mind open, and I want to hear more from you. For instance, if we're looking for something unusual, where do we find it? Do they live under that tomb?"

"They are or were in the dolmen," Greg said. "That's the only thing in the area that would feel like a safe hiding place to them. Of course, with all the people investigating, they may have decided that already and found another hideout."

"Lieutenant Billings," Lear said, "we all agree we need to pursue the investigation. If we excavate that dolmen, we'll either find positive evidence—that these things exist—or negative evidence—that there's nothing unusual. I'd like you to take charge of having it excavated."

"It's awfully big, sir," Billings said.

"You don't have to tear the whole thing up," Greg pointed out. "All we need is to get a backhoe to dig out a wedge into the center. But, for God's sake, have your people there with the heaviest guns you've got."

"I'd like to be there," Sporkin said.

"So would we," Julie added.

"Doctor, you have official capacity," Lear said. "Mr. Preston, Miss Sperling, you do not."

"If it is dangerous, that means no civilians," Billings said.

"You've been insisting there's no danger," Greg snapped.

"I don't know what the hell's happening, all right?" Billings said. "But when we investigate a crime scene, we keep control. No one there who doesn't have an official need to be there. We're keeping that thing cordoned off."

"Now I get it," Greg said with a little smile. "You're right, you don't know what's happening—or you don't want to admit it. Your concern is that if you do find something, you want to make sure you control access. Make sure people don't hear the LAPD is chasing something unbelievable. That's your concern."

"You're out of line, Mr. Preston," Lear said stiffly. "We have a responsibility to the people of this city. If there's something they need to know to protect themselves, we'll tell them, no matter what it makes us look like. But we're going to be damn sure what we tell them is accurate first. Lieutenant, can we get that excavation going tomorrow morning?"

"I'll see to it, sir."

"We're not going to get anywhere with more argument, so I'm going to close this meeting," Lear said. "Doctor, will you make up a briefing book with your photographs and test results? I don't know what to make of your findings, but I want them in a form I can show someone if I have to—just in case. You should send me the digital version, too, but there's something persuasive about old-fashioned hard copies."

"Now, to our two civilian witnesses," Lear said. "Whatever's going on, I'll concede you two are in danger."

"Why don't they stay at my apartment tonight, sir?" Fernandez suggested. "Detective Welles can stay with us, and it's quite secure."

"Excellent idea. And all four of you get some sleep. You look terrible. Meeting adjourned."

* * *

As they filed out of the room, Kerns fell in beside Greg. "I'd like to talk to you some more," he said quietly.

"Why?"

"Because you may be under police escort, but I'm not. And I want to find out what these creatures are."

Greg felt a chill. "They'll kill you."

"Greg—if I can call you Greg—I know I'm a bit out of shape, but I've collected dangerous animals in the wild all over the world. Maybe these aren't animals, properly speaking, but I still want to study them."

"What the hell can I say to convince you?" Greg asked. "You're crazy. These things kill anybody who gets near them!"

"Well, I'm going to keep in touch, anyway," Kerns said. "Whether we get them alive or dead, this is the chance of a lifetime—far more than that. Promise me you'll keep me updated."

"I would think Dr. Sporkin would do that."

Kerns frowned and lowered his voice further, eyeing the backs of the two cops walking just ahead. "John's a good man. But he works 'for the public good,' like everyone else here. Damn it; just keep me updated, right?"

Greg, Julie, and the detectives reached the glass doors of the building. Holding open the door, Greg turned back to Kerns.

"No promises, Doc."

"I may be able to help you, too, you know. Look, just give me your cell number."

"No."

"Then an email address for you, okay?"

Greg hesitated, then recited an address. "You can email. But I mean it—no promises."

The door closed with Kerns still inside. Julie turned to Greg. "I heard most of that. Is he that dedicated or that stupid?"

"I can't believe he really understands what we're saying if he wants to meet one of these things," Greg said. "Sure, a spectacular new species, one that doesn't even fit anywhere in the known animal kingdom—I can see him being willing to risk his life for that. Still, I wouldn't want to see one again if Kerns had it in his zoo behind six-inch bulletproof glass."

Fernandez's place turned out to be an apartment in an older building in the city's southwest area. Their route to the building led west on Exposition Boulevard, past the L.A.U. complex, and through neighborhoods where Welles suggested no "little monsters" were going to go. "This is Rollin' 30's territory," he said. "Those dwarves come through here without the right colors on, and all our problems are over."

Past Arlington Avenue, the mix of retail shops and apartment buildings turned a little more upscale. "Not really gang territory here. Or at least they're not very active," Welles said. "The gangs know Gary's in the neighborhood, so they all stay out."

They pulled into Fernandez' building, and the detective led them up to his second-floor apartment. It did have a balcony, which made Greg uneasy. On the other hand, it had iron grilles over the windows, plenty of security locks, and window air conditioners, so there were no vents. Greg supposed the crucifix in the entryway and the icon of Our Lady of Guadeloupe in the dining room couldn't hurt.

Greg and Julie settled in while Fernandez went out for groceries, and Welles made a cell call from the kitchen. "Yes, it's going to be all night," Greg heard him saying. "No, I can't get out of it. Look, you know…" There was silence. There had been an undercurrent of concern in the detective's voice.

When Welles came back in, Greg and Julie tried not to look at him, but he caught the atmosphere and grinned. "Don't read too much into that. My wife and I are great. But she's convinced if I die on the job, it's going to be guarding a witness. Ten years as a cop's wife, and she still believes the plots on *The Rookie*. I never heard of a cop killed guarding a witness."

It was growing dark when Fernandez came back. He apologized for the pile of frozen dinners he unpacked.

"Please, don't worry," Greg said. "We're the ones imposing on you, after all."

"It's not the first time I've played host for witnesses," Fernandez replied. "Besides, I like having someone to talk to. I'm between relationships, which is usually the case for me. Usually, I just listen to the neighbors fight and wonder if someone is going to bang on my door and ask me to settle it."

After dinner, they tried to make small talk, but the conversation inevitably turned back to the korrigans.

"How do you think those things are following you around?" Welles asked.

"Like I was thinking before, it has to be scent," Greg said. "Somewhere in that mockery of a face, there must be something that does what a nose does. We think one scent-marked Julie's car, but we haven't been using it. A tracking dog could still have followed us, couldn't it?"

"I think so," Welles said. "Some of those mutts are pretty amazing."

"It would seem they have impressive capabilities since it didn't help very much when you took the cab," Fernandez said. "It delayed them, apparently, but it didn't stop them completely."

"How do they work?" Julie asked, clearly unnerved by Fernandez's point. "I mean, is there just one group that goes out and then goes back to the dolmen, or do they have scouts or something following us and reporting back somehow?"

Greg shook his head. "It's hard to figure. I don't know what kind of communication they use. For all we know, they could be telepathic or even part of some group mind—like ants, but only more intelligent. That sounds pretty far-fetched, I know. My point is that these things are just so different we can't know anything for sure."

"And I thought we humans were perplexing," Fernandez said with a thin smile. "Now we may be contending with something that is hard to believe exists, but what makes it worse is that we don't even know how it thinks."

"Not entirely true," Welles said. "Yeah, it's completely alien—hell, maybe it's from outer space. But they do have an M.O. like everyone else. So far, we know they never attack in daylight. They'll use a weapon if it's handy but don't need one. They're good trackers, but not instantaneous ones."

"You sound like you believe in them now," Julie noted.

Welles grinned at her. "I don't see where I have much choice."

His face turned thoughtful. "It's different from dealing with your usual perps, though. There are two kinds of perps. Whether it's a mugger or a gangbanger, they're either smart or dumb. The dumb ones get caught easy because they make big mistakes. I had a guy— swear to God—write a robbery note to a bank teller once. He wrote on the back of an appointment slip for a meeting with his parole officer. Had his name on it.

"Your smart perps, at least the ones we catch, get caught for the same reason. They still make mistakes, but they make smaller mistakes, or put people between them and the crimes. So mistakes are harder to spot. Sooner or later, though, if they keep doing it and we keep on the case, someone makes a little slip.

"But we need to get smart enough about them to know a mistake when it happens."

They waited for the late news and scanned the local media's internet sites, but there was no word of the hotel incident.

"Figures," Welles observed. "In Los Angeles, a shotgun blast in a fancy hotel doesn't even rate a report."

"I think we ought to make a check outside," Fernandez said.

Welles considered it. "You're right, we should. Just a quick one. Keep close together."

"Are you sure that's a good idea?" Greg asked.

"I was in the Army," Welles said. "You always make sure your perimeter's secure."

Welles retrieved his shotgun and handed it to Greg. The two detectives slipped outside, coatless, holsters exposed, and sidearms loose. "Lock the door," Welles said.

Greg did, and he and Julie sat down to await the officers' return.

Minutes dragged past.

"Maybe we should have argued harder," Julie said.

"How would we have stopped them?"

"I don't know. I just got a bad feeling all of a sudden. Maybe—"

The crack of a pistol shot splintered the night.

17

Julie ran to the balcony door, pushing the curtain aside. "It was this way!"

"Julie, get down!" Greg grabbed her by the shoulder and yanked her away from the door. He pulled them both back to a red, overstuffed sofa and crouched behind it, clutching the shotgun hard. "Keep low! Don't let them see you!"

Breathing heavily, she squatted beside him. "Why just one shot?"

"Hopefully, he hit what he was aiming at."

"Or he missed, and it got him. Greg, we've got to help!"

"Alan said to stay put, so we stay. Hold on. I'll see if anything's visible." Ignoring his own instructions of a moment ago, Greg crept forward and nudged the edge of the curtain back with the shotgun muzzle. The balcony overlooked a poorly lit parking lot. Greg could see nothing moving.

"I don't see them," he reported.

"Greg, they might need help!"

"They're cops, Julie, they're not helpless. Our priority right now is to do what they told us and sit tight. They'll come back."

"What happens if they don't?"

"Then we call for help." Greg peered outside again. Still nothing.

They jumped as a knock sounded on the door. "It's all right, it's us!" came Welles' urgent voice.

Greg hurried to unlock the door. "What happened?"

Welles charged past him as Fernandez relocked the door. Welles was immediately on his cell phone to headquarters, demanding backup—and the coroner.

When he put the phone down, the others crowded around him. "Are you all right?" Julie asked.

"We're fine," Welles said. "But that moron from the zoo isn't. He's dead."

Julie pressed her hands to her face. "God, no. Not another one."

Greg put an arm around her and tried to calm his own heart's frantic beat.

"Where was he?" Greg asked.

"In a car in the parking lot. Must have tailed us. Damn it, we didn't watch for a tail because, hell, your little dwarves don't drive cars, so why would we? Kerns was sitting there watching the building, I guess. Stupid bastard had a tranquilizer gun. He wanted his zoo specimen, I guess.

"When we came out, we saw the movement in the car. Then— hell, I've got to sit down."

Julie shook Greg off and guided the stunned detective to a chair.

"Thanks," he said, his hand lingering on her arm. "Anyway, Gary yelled. Then this—thing—crawled out the car window. I didn't get that good a look. But I know now what scared you." He looked into Greg's eyes. "Just the size, the way it moved—I don't know what it was. But it sure as shit wasn't human."

He took in a long breath and let it out slowly. "It crawled out of the car and then just stood there a second. Gary took a shot. That's the really crazy part. He hit it. I know he did 'cause the round knocked it into the side of the car. And Gary doesn't miss. He's got a DE rating—Distinguished Expert—with the nine-mil. So the damn thing fell. Then it got up and ran away."

Welles lowered his gaze to the carpet, shaking his head. "Kerns was all torn up, like the rest of them. I've seen guys—crackheads—get up and run after they were shot. But something that small, and at that range...It ran perfectly normal. Normal for it, I guess I mean. Dammit, I mean what I'm trying to say is that it ran like it hadn't been touched. Just took off faster than hell. We lost it when it went around the building."

Welles shook himself, making a visible effort to regain his composure. "We've got to go out and wait where the body is. It might come back—or have friends. Let me borrow that shotgun. Gary has one in the bedroom that's loaded. Get that one and wait for us."

"All right. Sure you're okay?"

Welles nodded. "We'll be right back."

* * *

Greg and Julie watched from the balcony as a flock of police cars and ambulances gathered around the blue Impala that had become a coffin for Dr. Philip Kerns. There came the flashes from cameras, the murmur of detectives studying the scene, and finally, the body was loaded into an ambulance and driven away. Greg found himself actually being glad it was dark. He had no wish for a good look at Kerns' remains.

It was almost two hours after the gunshot when the detectives came back in, followed by Captain Lear. The tired, unsettled policemen slumped onto the sofa and chairs in the apartment.

"Four bodies," Lear mused. "The chief wants to see me in the morning. This is turning into another Grim Sleeper case."

"Captain, it's a hell of a lot worse than that," Welles said. "Because I've seen the killer myself now. And it's not a person."

Lear hesitated. "Detective, I've known you for a long time. I don't find this any easier to believe than I did before, but I have to accept your report. I do have to ask again, though. With Mr. Preston's speculations in your mind and in the dark, is there any possibility you could have been mistaken?"

Welles shook his head firmly. "No, sir. I wish to hell there was."

"I have to agree, Captain," Fernandez said. "Its size was like a chimpanzee, but the arms were shorter. The way it ran wasn't human at all. It bounded, though it kept bending forward a little. I saw it put a hand down once for more spring before it jumped over a wall. It was very powerful—in other words, an animal."

Lear nodded. "All right. Like I said, I have to accept your report. But the chief isn't going to buy it without more evidence."

"Like a body," Welles said.

"Like that. You've got to think about how unbelievable this is. You're saying an unknown type of animal has committed four murders, maybe five, in the city of Los Angeles. More than that, it's an animal that, on two occasions, was shot at close range and apparently survived. No matter how much faith I have in you, the higher-ups are likely to grasp any possibility—even that you are crazy or on drugs. You have to understand that no rational human will accept this unless the evidence is undeniable."

"You did," Welles pointed out.

Lear smiled grimly. "I'm three months from retirement."

He paused again, tapping his fingertips together, then went on. "There will probably be a task force created for this case. Assistant Chief Henderson will likely be the head man, but you two are my aces. You've seen more and know more than anyone else. You're now a special detail reporting directly to me. You're relieved of all other cases. You need to tackle this while also keeping Mr. Preston and Ms. Sperling safe. If you think it's wise to change locations every night, I'll arrange for it."

Welles shook his head. "However they find us, they do it fast," he said. "In fact, they seem to do it faster every time."

"That would make sense," Greg said. "The more familiar they are with our scent, the easier we are to track."

"All right. I can convince the boss there's a crazed and bizarre killer—or killers—on the loose, and we have to plan a hunt. I'll tell him what you think you saw, but he will still think we're dealing with humans. Proving that we aren't is going to be a job for you two."

Welles and Fernandez exchanged speculative looks. "Well, sir, we'll kick that ball as hard as we can," Fernandez said.

"Sit tight until morning," Lear said. "This building will be watched, just in case. Then, get down to where they'll be digging up that tomb. I'll be a little busy myself, but I'll make sure they let you in. Mr. Preston, I've decided I want you there. You're the expert on these things."

"No one's an expert, Captain."

"Well, you're the closest thing we've got. Consider yourself drafted."

* * *

When the captain left, the others continued to discuss the situation.

"Where do you think they are in the city?" Welles asked Greg.

"Could be almost anywhere. According to legend, they lived in caves when they weren't using tunnels under dolmens. I'd say they'd look for similar hideouts. Sewers would be likely—they could not only stay out of the light but move undetected. They seem to have very good navigational instincts. Consider the way they can go through air-conditioning ducts to a specific apartment.

"I'm sure it comes back to scent trails. They follow our scent, go down into the sewers when necessary, then come up at night."

"Isn't there any way of throwing them off?" Julie asked.

"I've read of a mixture used in World War II to throw off tracking dogs," Greg said. "I doubt if we could get our hands on cocaine and dried blood, though."

"I'd hate to have to bust myself for possession," Welles said. "Besides, these things are so weird they might eat cocaine, for all we know."

Fernandez glanced at his watch. "It's getting late," he said. "Alan, why don't you rest? I'll take the first watch."

"Okay," Welles yawned. "I should argue, but I'm too tired. Wake me in two hours, and we'll trade off."

Welles lay down in the bedroom. The others stayed up a little, with Julie engaging Fernandez in a discussion of the Catholic iconography in his apartment.

"I used to love the Church, the crucifix, and all of the symbolism," she said. "It was so solid, something that would last forever, and you could hold onto. I just sort of drifted away a little at a time. What about you?"

"As the Protestants would put it, I still cling to the old rugged cross," he said. "Truth *is* eternal."

"But with all you see as a detective, all the deaths and the child abuse and all that," Julie said, "How do you hold on to God being good and in charge?"

Greg perked up an eyebrow. He'd wondered a bit about God the last few days.

"It's not incongruous," Fernandez said. "Remember, the Church teaches that this is a fallen world. Satan has free rein here to try to influence the minds of men. It is depressing how good he is at it. But his power is not eternal. God's is."

Greg was impressed by Fernandez' certainty. Impressed and, he admitted to himself, a little envious.

"I hope that's true," Julie said.

Finally, Greg and Julie settled in on the sleeper sofa in the living room. Fernandez settled in his recliner, cradling a cup of coffee in both hands, his shotgun resting across his knees. Julie groped for Greg's hand under the bedspread draped over the sleeper and held it tightly.

In the early morning, they were on the move again. A call from headquarters told Welles the excavation would start at nine o'clock.

"I think I've started appreciating sunrises a lot more," Julie commented as they left the apartment building.

"As opposed to college days, you mean?" Greg smiled. "You thought scheduling a class before nine-thirty violated the laws of nature."

"The things we're hunting—or that are hunting us—are the offense against nature," Welles said. "They won't even die."

"They'll die," Greg said. "The one I shot at the hotel may be dead, for all we know. It just takes a lot of firepower."

"I've always been fine with the Glock seventeen, but we can buy forty-fives if we don't think a nine-millimeter is enough," Welles said. "I always thought that was silly—if you can't take out a target with a nine-mil, you have no business shooting at it. Only the SWAT guys insist on having forty-fives. Well, now I'm going to get a forty-five the first chance I get."

"He certainly has the nine hundred dollars to spare," Fernandez said to Greg and Julie. "He's worn the same sport coat since he made detective."

Welles glared at his partner, but with a grin, and then turned to Greg. "Write that down. Gary made his first joke about me in three years of being partners."

The group walking to Welles' car already had two Glock nine-millimeter pistols and two shotguns between them, plus the backup .32 revolver Welles kept in an ankle holster. The detectives had reviewed the operation of all the weapons with Greg and Julie the night before. The two civilians both carried pepper spray, which Greg was more convinced than ever would be effective, but the short range of the spray made them uncomfortable. He'd asked Welles about a gun.

"I've never in my whole career tried to get a gun permit for a witness we were protecting," Welles said. "If we can't protect them, then they're screwed anyway. But this case is so freaking scary and weird—what's your experience with handguns?"

"All my life until college," Greg said. "We were pretty rural in Pinecotton, Arizona. When I wasn't using a shotgun, I hunted rabbits and cleared out rattlesnakes with a pistol. Usually, a twenty-two semi-auto or a thirty-eight revolver. I got good at snap shots."

"I'll ask the boss," Welles said. "Maybe it'll be okay if we can work some training in."

Greg found himself getting more nervous the closer they got to the museum. Were the korrigans, at least some of them, still there? It made sense to think they were. All the victims had been killed away from the tomb except for Windsor, and he was the only one whose body had been hidden. That might show a conscious attempt to keep attention away from the dolmen itself.

"Greg, where do you think these things came from? Originally, I mean?" Julie asked.

Greg was aware of the two detectives in the front seat, straining to hear his answer.

"They're so different from anything else in the world that it's hard to see how they could have evolved here, although I suppose I can't say it a hundred percent. If they're not from Earth, there are two things I can think of, both of them way-out."

"Everything about this mess is way-out," Welles said. "Give it a shot."

"All right. First, some kind of tiny embryo egg could have come here from elsewhere by accident. A meteorite fell near Orgeuil, France, in 1868. In the 1960s, two chemists claimed they could identify fossils of five types of microscopic life forms from inside it."

"It's funny. I never heard of that," Julie said.

"It was published but disputed. There are also several reports of landed UFOs that describe small, hairy dwarfs. I've never taken UFOs seriously. But I'm starting to wonder now."

"You're right," Welles said. "They're both way out there."

"You asked."

"Both your ideas might be right, in a way," Julie said. "Maybe some space microbe came down millions of years ago, then evolved into these things."

Greg nodded. "Right now, I'd say anything's possible. If we can nail these things and kill one—or capture it—the tests on it are going to be interesting. *Real* interesting."

* * *

At the museum, the cop at the gate glanced at the detectives' badges and waved them through. To Greg, the man looked a little strung out.

Welles parked within sight of the museum house, and the group walked on. Both detectives carried shotguns.

A yellow front-end loader was revving up next to the dolmen when they came around the house. A small crowd of uniformed and non-uniformed cops was gathered around it. Greg recognized Lt. Billings and Dr. Sporkin.

"Let's go join the party," Welles said.

Billings saw them coming and scowled. "Detective, what are these two—?"

"Captain's orders," Welles said, without even acknowledging Billings' rank. "I'm sure you heard we had another killing last night."

"I did. I heard you saw the killer but didn't catch him."

"Most suspects don't get up and run away after they've been shot."

Billings seemed to be trying to devise a suitable comeback for a moment, but gave up. "Just keep your wits out of the way," he finally said.

Greg turned to Welles. "He thinks I'm a wit now?"

"Short for 'witness,' Genius."

"Damn. I thought he was starting to appreciate me."

The loader had already dug out or shoved aside one of the large stone slabs surrounding the tomb's exterior. Now its diesel engine chugged to full power, and the teeth of its steel scoop bit deep into the earthen body of the dolmen.

Sporkin came over to stand beside Greg. "Do you think we'll find your korrigans?"

"I don't know." Greg looked again at the havoc being wreaked on the tomb. "It'll be a while yet before we find out. They have a lot of dirt to go through, and then they'll have to break into the burial chamber in the middle. Wait 'til the British government and the archaeologists find out what we're doing to this thing now."

"With Windsor gone, I don't know what'll happen with that," Julie said. "Probably, they'll get a court order to ship it back to England."

The loader was now building a pile of soil next to the increasingly large chunk it was eating out of the dolmen. Greg and the others edged closer, inspecting the detritus as the machine charged back for its next load.

"I don't see anything yet," Sporkin said. "How were these structures laid out?"

"The chamber in the middle will be made with stones," Greg said.

"Some dolmens had a tunnel running to the outside. The design varied depending on the area and the time period. I haven't talked to anyone who actually did the reconstruction of this thing. I should have thought of that, but it's too late now."

The loader ripped even deeper into the dolmen, hauling out earth in a wedge-shaped pattern as it dug toward the center of the mound. It was a typical August Saturday, and the observers sweated and wiped their brows as they watched the work continue.

The sun had crept considerably higher by the time it happened. As usual, the loader operator drove into the cut, then abruptly backed out without picking up any dirt. He pulled further away from the dolmen and shut down his machine.

"I've hit something!" he shouted.

18

The group of onlookers edged forward. Several of the cops had shovels, and Billings waved them into the wedge dug out of the dolmen. The others followed close behind.

The officers dug into the chalky soil. Almost immediately, one man gave a shout.

"Well, I just lost my shovel," he said, pointing to a dark hole in front of him. "Either it got eaten by a monster, or there's a tunnel here."

"Widen that hole!" Billings said. "The rest of you keep your guns at the ready!"

Somewhat apprehensively, two cops stuck their shovels into the hole and tried to widen it.

"It's rock on both sides!" one called.

Greg stepped beside Billings. "That's the burial chamber," he said. "Listen, it's probably not very stable. Don't open up the hole any more than you have to."

"Let's try this," Billings said to his men. "Dig out a little around those rocks and see if we can get a cable around one of them."

A half-hour of sweaty work later, a cable was looped around one end of a desk-sized stone. The other end was hitched to the loader, and the machine revved up once more.

"Gently!" Greg called to the machine operator. "Just pull it enough to widen the hole a little!"

The guy nodded. Billings shot Greg a hard look but again said nothing.

The loader gave a backward lurch, and the darkness widened from a slit to an opening about two feet across. Billings waved his hand, and the operator cut his engine. Greg was staring at the hole. Nothing was moving.

A cop holding a shotgun in front of him edged to the mouth of the cavity and looked in.

"Don't see anything!" he called. "Give me a light!"

A flashlight was passed in. The cop stuck most of his body through the hole, then popped back out a moment later.

"There's nobody in here. Just a little room!"

"Let me look for myself," Billings said. The lieutenant took the flashlight, knelt at the hole, and wriggled in. He came out a moment later and stood up, brushing dirt off his shirt and glaring at Greg.

"Ain't nobody in here but us monsters."

* * *

Greg and Julie exchanged helpless looks.

"What now?" Welles asked.

"Let me take a look," Greg said.

"Be my guest." Billings almost bowed as he handed over the flashlight. Greg silently asked his claustrophobia to take it easy, and he crept on his knees into the hole.

The chamber was about six feet across. The walls were rough stones, well fitted together. Greg's immediate thought was that the space was too neat. There should be something in the dolmen—droppings, footprints, some trace of korrigan habitation. He looked at the floor. It seemed unnaturally smooth. More dirt should have sifted down between the stones. Were korrigans smart enough to sweep out their traces when they moved?

Greg looked around again, but if the korrigans had cleaned up, they had been very thorough. Pretty impressive job in total darkness, he thought. Greg's nerves started shooting alarm signals through his body, and he scrambled for the opening.

He went too fast, slipping on the dirt, and his right foot kicked hard against a stone slab—which moved. Not much, just a hair, but Greg ignored his discomfort and pushed at the stone with his hands. It moved further, sliding away from him into the earth, and Greg yanked his arms back and flung himself out through the entrance hole.

Out in the sunlight, Greg leaned against the dolmen, gulping air. Julie and a cop gathered close, giving him concerned looks.

"Greg, are you all right?" Julie asked.

He managed a shaky grin. "Forgot how much I hate small spaces." He pointed back into the hole. "Lieutenant, there's a hole in there—one of those slabs is just propped up, not supporting the ceiling at all. My hands shoved it back easy. Right on this side of the entrance. It's a tunnel."

"Your hands seem to end up in a lot of places lately," Julie said.

Greg puzzled a second, trying to think why she would make a reference to their making love, and then his still-spinning brain grasped that she was referring to the finding of Windsor's body. He just nodded.

"How do you know it's a tunnel? Or anything?" Billings demanded.

"Because I expected it to be there. I mentioned to Detective Welles that there are tunnels all over Europe they call erdstall or schrazelloch, which means 'goblin holes.' There's no agreement on who made them or why."

"Goblin holes." Billings shook his head but went to look into the excavation again.

Billings peered at the hole, then shrugged and gestured at two shovel-bearing officers. "Take a look, you guys."

The two men slid past Greg and went in.

Only a moment later, one man popped his head out. "Lieutenant, he's right! It's a little tunnel!"

"So it's big enough to crawl through?" Billings asked.

"A little guy might be able to. But I'd hate to try it."

Billings nodded. "Well, we've come this far. Let's see where it goes. Bring up the dog."

A uniformed handler with an alert-looking German shepherd appeared. "See if you can get your boy to go through that tunnel," Billings said. "We'll spread the guys out so they can see where he pops up."

"Yes, sir. Come on, Buckeye! C'mon, boy!" The handler nudged the dog toward the hole leading into the burial chamber.

Buckeye halted, sniffing energetically. Then his head snapped up, and he growled, a sound that came from deep in his chest and sent a shiver through Greg's body. *He knows*, Greg realized, the hair standing up on his own neck. *The dog knows.* Somehow, through a thousand years of breeding, training, and civilization, some part of the dog's brain carried the memory of this scent, and he did not like it. The primeval wolf-growl rumbled out again, louder, and the shepherd bared its teeth at the entrance to the dolmen.

Buckeye plunged into the chamber. The handler looked in after him. "He's gone in the hole!"

"Okay, big circle, everybody!" Billings called. "Watch for where the dog comes out!"

"If he comes out," Julie whispered.

* * *

The dog did come out. He burst from a hole hidden in the densely-planted brush surmounting an earthen bank about forty yards from the dolmen. Buckeye barked furiously, his head swinging around, repeatedly pushing his snout at the ground as if trying to find a scent he'd lost.

Greg and the others converged on the tunnel exit. Branches,

clearly arranged on purpose, concealed the opening. Like the burial chamber, the part of the tunnel they could look into showed no signs of footprints or other evidence.

"Where do you think they are now?" Julie asked.

"Like we were talking about before, I'll bet they went into a sewer," Greg said. "Or maybe a basement if they found an abandoned building."

"So what do we do now, hotshot?" Billings demanded.

Greg studied the opening again. "They're smarter than I thought," he said. "That's a good trick, brushing out their traces. Now, they could be anywhere in the basin."

"Or nowhere," Billings snorted. "For all I know, kids made this tunnel."

The suggestion that children had dug a tunnel half the length of a football field on a patrolled estate without being seen was so absurd Greg couldn't think of a reply.

"All right, let's seal up this hole," Billings told his men. "It's a safety hazard. Then let's pack up and get out of here."

Greg turned to Sporkin. "Well, what do you say, Doc?"

"The evidence we had is still there, but I'm disappointed. I don't think you'll prove your case to the people who matter until you have a body."

"Damn it, can't you make people listen? These things are hunting us, Doctor. I don't want the next bodies you see to be ours!"

"I'll do what I can," Sporkin said.

"Greg, is there any reason to stay here?" Welles asked.

"I guess not. Billings' mind was opening up a little, but he managed to close it again."

"If it's just us, then we'll have to do." Welles gave a little shrug, and the foursome began the walk back to the car. "How many of these things do you suppose there are, anyway?"

Greg shook his head. "No way to be sure. Not many, though, or they'd have needed more victims and a bigger hideaway by now."

"I was wondering about that," the detective said. "I remember somebody in the department telling me the missing-persons reports were up this summer from last year. Not a lot, but enough so somebody noticed. The COMPSTAT guys should be able to break down how many were in this area. We can check with Open-Unsolved to make sure nothing has already been sent to them."

"Do it," Greg urged. "We need to chase any possibility that might give us clues to their whereabouts." He paused as he remembered what he'd seen from the freeways. "I'd think they'd be preying on the homeless camps," he said.

Welles rubbed his chin. "Yeah. I can think of two reasons why we might now see that. First, the population is transient and a lot of people are afraid of us, so maybe we don't get the information, People just assume someone moved on. Two is that there's something they don't like about those camps. Too many people, or too many sick people, or whatever. But we should check."

"I volunteer Saturday mornings at the LSU—Legal Services for the Unhoused," Julie said. "I can start asking questions too."

Greg's eyebrows went up. "I didn't know that."

"I'm not a crusader, but I have to do something," she said. "It's a lot worse than when you and I volunteered at the community service center they ran at LAU."

"Maybe I need to think about that," Greg said. "I've got a nice house in a nice town in Durham. I make donations, but I've gotten disengaged."

"You've always been a good man," she said softly. "But maybe you have."

They reached the car and climbed in for the drive back downtown. Welles cranked the wheezing air conditioner up to full. Greg and Julie slumped in the back, drained by the morning's letdown and the continuing fatigue of fear.

"So, how do we look for these things?" Fernandez asked. "We can't go around asking who's seen little black dwarves."

"Plotting the disappearances might be a start," Welles said. "At least it might tell us where to look."

"It might," Greg said. "Or they might be smart enough to spread out, never take victims from the same area twice. Still, it's better than a wild guess. And they grew so fast they must have needed a lot of nutrition. They couldn't have been too picky."

"What about tracking them with dogs?" Julie asked.

"Nice idea," Welles said. "But remember, that dog this morning lost them as soon as they went out of their tunnel."

"They must not have much natural scent," Greg guessed. "It's only strong when they've been in one place a lot."

All were quiet for a minute. Then Greg forced himself to say what he'd been trying not to even think.

"We all know what we're avoiding mention of," he said quietly.

"What's that?" Welles asked.

"We don't need to track them down. They'll come for us."

"I haven't said it for a reason," Welles said. "Our job is to protect you. Don't even think about what I think you're thinking. As bad as I want these things, assuming they're real and I haven't gone nuts, that doesn't include using people as bait."

"You don't have a choice," Greg said. "There's no other way to catch them. Put Julie somewhere safe, under guard. Then put me where I'll be easy to find."

"No!" Julie snapped. "Greg, you can't do that."

"I didn't say I wanted to," Greg said, trying not to show how much his own idea terrified him. "I said we don't have a choice, and as much as I wish I were wrong, I'm not."

"No way in hell," Welles said. "We'll get the disappearance reports and try to narrow it down from there."

Greg gave up with a little nod. But he couldn't push the thought out of his mind.

They spent much of the afternoon at PAB again, the two witnesses killing time and studying internet sites, trading tidbits of folklore and supposition while the detectives filled out reports and went through the procedures required any time an officer fired his gun.

"What are you going to put as the reason for shooting?" Greg asked Fernandez.

"The truth," the detective replied. "I'll be very interested in seeing what reaction it gets."

"Professional Standards will want us sent for psych evals," Welles said. He grinned. "Wouldn't be the first time for me."

Welles went back to the coroner's to attend the autopsy on Kerns. He returned with nothing they could use. Kerns had been torn up like the other victims, although there were no bone punctures. There was also nothing unique that would add to their evidence.

"I talked to Lear, too," he said. "It went with the boss about like he expected. Lear can pull whatever resources he needs to solve the murders, but he'd better not come in again talking about weird animals unless he's got one in a box. By the way, nothing on McGraw. If they grabbed him, they cleaned up good."

When evening approached, they returned to Fernandez' apartment. None liked going back to a place the korrigans knew about, but they all agreed with Welles that moving around didn't help. It was better to make a stand on well-known ground.

"Some friends of ours will be in the neighborhood," Fernandez said. "In the Department, we look out for each other."

They drove to the apartment and settled in for another night. Greg wandered into the kitchen for a drink and found Welles measuring out a libation of his own. Welles had poured a tall glass of cola and now added a very small shot of rum to it.

"Can't indulge much in the good stuff at a time like this," Welles said. "Want one?"

"Just with the cola," Greg said. "I could use the rum part, but I might not stop."

Welles poured it for him. "You know, you're doing a good job for someone who just got dumped into the weirdest damn situation I ever saw."

"That's quite a compliment."

"I was in the Gulf War. Infantry. One thing I learned is that you size guys up pretty fast under fire. You've shown a lot of guts. I'm glad the Counselor has you around."

"Just doing what I can."

"No surprise there."

"I'm not sure what you mean."

"You guys have a history that's more than friends. I can read it plain as day."

"That was back in college. A long time ago."

"So it's just friends now?"

Greg flashed back to the night in the hotel. "Yes."

Welles nodded. "You can keep telling yourself that if you want to."

* * *

They slept as they had the night before, with all the lights on and the detectives taking turns standing guard. Greg repeatedly awoke, often with his heart racing from a nightmare. He stared at the locked patio doors and the barred windows and wondered how long a night could be.

In the end, though, the night did pass. Dawn seeped into the apartment, and the foursome rose, tired yet energized by the gratitude they all felt at still being alive.

"Happy Sunday morning," Greg said. "I don't think we'll make it to church today."

"Nope," Welles said. "By the way, I forgot to mention Lear dragged in the computer geeks yesterday and put them on the missing person's stuff. Maybe they'll see a pattern. Should have done that at the start."

"Speaking of patterns," Greg said, "it's clear now I was right about the killings all being connected, but the differences in Walt's killing still bother me."

"Don't get thrown off," Welles said. "In any kind of case, the puzzle pieces never fit a hundred percent. Real life is messy. A guy takes a different route to work one time, a woman changes her hair color, a guy grabs his backup gun instead of his usual one, and you get sent spinning off in a different direction. Even animals change their habits, right, or do different things from one animal to the next?"

"They do. One chimp will make a tool, while another one will just sit there, unable to understand. One gorilla will recognize himself in a mirror, another won't." Greg stopped for a moment, then looked hard at Welles. "Apes will experiment. If a chimp finds a new object, he'll pick it up, play with it, see what use he can put it to."

"The knife."

"Exactly. The korrigan saw a sharp object, picked it up, and tried it out."

"And that sent us on the wrong track. Like I said. Ninety percent fit is the best things ever get in this business."

"I wonder why they didn't come after us last night."

"Maybe they expected us to have moved again," Julie said.

"Could be," Welles said. "Or they knew we'd be alert, and they've learned something about guns."

Welles' cell phone vibrated. He listened a moment, said, "Yeah," and put it down with a suddenly-shaky hand. He spoke to the others without turning to face them.

"Lear's dead."

19

G reg stared at Welles, feeling like he'd been kicked hard in the gut.

Welles turned slowly toward the others. "Hit and run driver. Outside his own house," he said in a lifeless voice.

"Then it wasn't the korrigans?" Julie asked.

Welles fumbled for a kitchen chair and sat down. "All they know is he was run over in the street in front of his house real late last night. Guess he'd stayed late at headquarters. Whatever bastard hit him never even stopped."

"He could have been pushed," Greg said.

"Come on," Welles replied, a little animation creeping back into his voice. "An armed cop is gonna let one of those little things throw him out in the street? It was a crazy freakin' accident, that's all."

"You're fooling yourself—or you're trying to," Greg said firmly. "You're too smart not to think of it. Why would a man step out in the street in front of his house in the middle of the night?"

"Hell, I don't know! And neither do you!" Welles snapped. He started to go on but stopped, shaking his head. "Hell, I knew Lear from Rampart. He was one of the best. Best cops, best captains, best everything." Welles picked up a kitchen knife, toyed with it, then jabbed it hard into a wooden cutting board. "God damn, if they could get him, they could get any of us." He looked up. "Gary, let's get the hell out of here."

* * *

The ritual of passing time at police headquarters was becoming frighteningly familiar and agonizingly slow. Greg and Julie settled into the cubicle beside the detectives' home base. Julie checked office email on her smartphone— "Can't break the habit," she said—while Greg set up his laptop and started typing.

"What are you writing?" Julie asked.

"Everything I know. Everything we've seen so far," Greg said.

"Didn't you promise no writing?"

"I'm not writing for an article or a book," Greg said. "I'm writing because we know more than anyone else, and we want as complete a record as we can leave for people who study these things later. I'd appreciate it if you'd look over what I've got in a little bit."

"Don't you dare tell me you're writing it down in case we don't live," Julie said.

Greg's hands tensed, and his fingers paused on the keys.

"I'm writing it because memories are fallible," he finally said. "No one, not even me, remembers every detail."

Her lips tightened for a moment. "You didn't answer my question."

"Technically, Counselor, you didn't ask one."

She made no reply.

Twice the detectives left to check out reports: one missing person, one murder. Neither turned out to be related.

"Dumbest murder I ever saw," Welles said when the detectives filed back in after the last expedition. "Little alley behind 29thh Street. Perp used a knife, but he left it in the victim in plain sight. Then the perp trips on the curb running away and knocks himself out."

"Why did you get called on it at all?" Greg asked.

"Standing orders to everybody are that we get called on any one-eighty-seven done with a knife or an unknown weapon. Nothing for us to do except swear when I got back to my car and found some dog had peed on it."

"Alan," Julie said sharply before Greg could process the point. "Are you sure it was a dog?"

"Why?"

"Remember Greg told you something marked my car?"

"Shit," Welles said. "We didn't see the dog, no. Come to think of it, it didn't smell like one, either."

"We should ask SID to take a swab," Fernandez said. "And take my car home."

"They didn't set that up just to pee on my car," Welles protested.

"I doubt it," Greg said. "Target of opportunity, maybe. They were sniffing for you, and they just got lucky."

"I'm sick of them being the lucky ones," Julie said.

"Agreed, Counselor," Welles replied. "We need to give them some bad luck for a change."

Welles dug into the missing-person stats while Fernandez spent the afternoon on Google Earth and two other imaging services, studying every location involved in the case. So far, nothing useful was emerging. Julie called and messaged her contacts at the LSU, asking cautiously about reports of unusual disappearances and begging for discretion.

"At least one thing is going to come out of Captain Lear being killed," Julie said to Greg.

"What's that?"

"There have been people killed already, but he's the first cop. The whole department's going to be on a war footing. Killing a cop in this department is like wounding a lion. Everyone's going to make this a priority until they get justice. Or vengeance."

"Right now, either will do."

Welles interrupted them. "We're going to go over to the lab to check on things about Lear for ourselves," the detective said. "Back in a few minutes."

Greg nodded. Julie did, too, but almost uninterestedly as if her last comment had spent all her thoughts. Greg looked closely at her. Julie now sat with her eyes closed, her face expressionless. He wondered if she needed to see a psychiatrist again. She'd been taking shock after shock. No matter how strong she was, it had to be too much to handle at some point.

No, not yet. He wasn't going to voice any such idea right now. Clinics were hardly secure places. *Besides, I might be the one to crack first.*

Eventually, Welles and Fernandez came back, wearing the grim expressions seen on battle-weary soldiers. Welles sank into his chair and swiveled to look at the two witnesses.

"We don't know," he said.

"Don't know what?" Greg prodded.

"Don't know that he was murdered. All we have is that he was run over by something with a high bumper—pickup truck, most likely— and it had some red paint. They found a chip of it on his gun. Lab will try to match the paint to a car. But the only injuries are from the impact. We called the coroner, too. The vehicle wasn't going very fast, but fast enough to throw him against the curb and break his neck."

Greg noted the hardened cop couldn't seem to bring himself to use Lear's name.

Welles shrugged. "No witnesses. He was here late, and he would have gotten home around midnight. We figure it happened right after that. Everyone's just waiting for that lab report so we can try to nail the vehicle."

"That's not the damn point," Greg insisted. "It's not what hit him. It's why he was there to get hit at all!"

"I know, I know. He parked his car in the drive next to his house. He never went in. Instead, he stepped into the street."

Julie was more attentive now. "So, he was chased," she said. The hand that held Greg's was trembling. "Maybe they jumped at him, and he freaked and ran."

Welles shook his head. "He was a nineteen-year cop."

"But he was only human," Greg said. "Alan, you've seen one in the dark. I've seen the thing right in the face. Trust me, anyone would panic."

"Lear wouldn't. Hell, you didn't."

"The hell I didn't. I've never been so scared in my life. I only shot because I already had the gun in my hands, and it was already pointed in the right direction. I couldn't think to aim or anything else. And I already believed in them. What if you were out in a boat, and a fifty-foot sea monster popped up, trying to eat you? Would you think rationally?"

"All right, all right. Hell, don't go dragging sea monsters into this. But don't let me hear you say Lear panicked again. If it was one of them, it was so close he didn't have time to pull. Let's grab a bite while we wait on the paint report."

The lab report came in by phone a few minutes later. The vehicle was a 2010 Ford F150 full-size pickup. The detectives scrambled to cross-check with the Department of Motor Vehicles, starting with the question of how many such trucks might be registered in or anywhere near Lear's Culver City neighborhood.

"You're still working the wrong end," Greg insisted as the detectives discussed the plans for truck-hunting.

"You got a better idea?" Welles asked.

"Maybe you're both wrong," Julie said.

Both men looked at her quizzically.

"Well, think about it," she said, turning first to Greg. "I agree this is so suspicious that it's not a coincidence. I'd bet anything those damn animals were involved. But think like a cop, Alan." She faced the detective. "Motive. Why would they be involved in Captain Lear's death?"

"I'm not sure what you mean. They chase everyone who gets near them—" he stopped. "But Lear never was near them."

"If they were following us, watching us, they would have seen him with us," Greg said. "But he wasn't close to them like Julie and I have been. And the way Walt, Rob Martin, and McGraw must have been at the estate."

"He was our leader," Welles said. "God, are they *that* intelligent? Could they have actually figured out he was leading us?"

Greg thought a moment. "If a new wolf wants to take over the pack, he picks out the alpha male," he said. "If they watched us that night we left the morgue, they wouldn't necessarily have to be smart. Lear was used to being in authority. He carried himself that way. Still, Culver City is what, ten miles? That's a long trip for animals we think are more sprinters than marathoners."

"We know they were in Griffith Park at the museum," Julie pointed out. "They traveled almost that far to show up downtown. If you're determined enough, you can hike a long way."

"So I don't think we're working the wrong end," Welles said. "We can't haul these things in for questioning. So we find the driver, we find out what he saw."

Greg nodded. "Okay. You're right."

"First time I think I've heard that from you since we met," Welles said. "Look, you're the expert. But I'm the guy whose job this is, and it's my captain and my friend who's dead. Your job is to look after each other and tell us anything you think is useful. And we'll try to look after you and exterminate these oversized cockroaches at the same time. Understand?"

Greg nodded.

"Greg, I'm going to show you a form on the computer. You have pistol experience, so I'll try for an emergency permit. I was right to trust you with the shotgun. I'll get you a handgun, but I tell you when you can carry it. And you keep it in the holster unless there are no cops left around and no other choice. Clear?"

"Clear."

"Julie, you'll have to make do with the pepper spray."

"I'm more comfortable with that anyway," she said.

"Okay, we'll be right back, so don't worry about us."

* * *

"Back to the waiting," Julie sighed. "This place is starting to drive me crazy."

"Let's not use that word," Greg said. "At least we're safe here. As safe as we would be anywhere."

"Being safe isn't enough. Pardon my cliché, but I feel like I'm still in a bad dream and I just want to wake up."

* * *

The day closed with no news, either of korrigans or pickup trucks.

"We checked all the trucks like that in the L.A. Basin, just about," Welles reported. "We'll be widening the search now. Every cop in Southern California is looking for that truck. We'll find it."

He gave Julie a tender look. "Hang in there, Counselor. I know this means at least one more night with the danger still out there. But we will get you through this all right."

"I know you'll do your best. Where are we going for the night?"

"Back to Gary's again. Like I said last night, don't worry. There'll be plenty of cops around."

"I wonder if these korrigans can live long in smog," Fernandez said. "They can't have gotten used to it in the time they lived in England."

"The trouble is, we just don't know what they can adapt to," Greg said. "Maybe carbon monoxide is poison—I hope so. But maybe not. Legend doesn't really say anything about what might kill them or what they're afraid of."

"What all this boils down to," Welles said, "is that we still don't know –"

Julie interrupted the officer. "That's not good enough! This is not about zoology class. This is about life and death."

Hernandez gave her a polite nod. "We all understand that, Ms. Sperling."

"No, you don't!"

Julie shot her hand into the doughnut box and came up with a raspberry-filled long john.

"This is your body." She snapped her hand closed, and red filling erupted from the destroyed pastry, dripping all over her hand and the desktop. "This is your body on monsters. Any questions?"

Welles was visibly riled if only a tiny, controlled bit. "Well, what's your idea?"

"There's an approach Tom Cooley at the law firm taught me," Julie said. "If you don't know what the opposing counsel is doing, look at what he's not doing. What witnesses could he call that are not on his list, or what evidence could he introduce that he doesn't? Figuring that out gives you insight into what he's thinking."

"For example?" Welles asked.

"Think of what they haven't done so far. They don't come out in the day, they don't show themselves, and they don't always tear up and eat their victims. My guess would be that means they're not desperate for food. They're finding enough somewhere. And if that's the case, we don't know yet if they can't stand the light or just prefer the night for concealment."

"Good thinking," Greg said. "Since we don't know how smart they are, we should err on the side of caution. Maybe we should think of them as primitive humans—like one of those lost tribes from the Amazon dropped into this environment. They've been reacting pretty much like some human tribes would in their situation. Hide as much as possible, move at night when you have to move and kill anyone who finds out about you. Just try to survive."

"You almost sound like you feel sorry for them," Julie said indignantly.

"No, not sorry. They killed my best friend, and they tried to kill you. I'm saying I think I basically understand why they act the way they do."

"So what do you think they'll do next?" Welles asked. "What would a lost bunch of Brazilian Indians, or whatever, try to do?"

"One of two things. Either keep trying to kill us or clear out of the area and find a place away from people."

"If they killed Captain Lear, they haven't cleared out," Welles said. "You're so damn cheerful I don't know how I stand it." He held out a holster with a nine-millimeter Glock 17 pistol. "Don't make me regret this."

* * *

They drove south on Sepulveda Boulevard, then turned west toward Fernandez's neighborhood.

"Two blocks to home base," Fernandez announced. "When we get there, everyone should stay—"

The crash jarred Greg hard against his seat belt. He grabbed for support as the car swerved crazily, all its occupants shouting at once. Then came another crash from the front this time, and Greg's skull slammed into the headrest on the back of the driver's seat.

Dazed, Greg mumbled an incoherent question as the car slid to a bumping halt. He knew they'd stopped, but the vehicle still seemed to be spinning around him. He felt Julie open his seat belt and grab his arm amid a nonsensical whirl of shouts and glass-breaking noises.

Greg fought to clear his head, but what filtered through his senses still seemed disjointed. Welles was yelling something, holding a pistol in his left hand. With his right, he was yanking at the shoulder of his partner, who didn't seem to be moving—or breathing.

"We've got to get out of here!" Julie shouted.

Glass broke again, louder. A dark, stubby arm was reaching through the rear window, clawing at them.

Somehow, Greg found himself outside the car. Julie was with him, as was Welles, who was aiming his pistol at the shattered carcass of his car.

"Move!" the cop shouted. "That way!" He pointed at the dimly visible mouth of an alley between two shuttered rows of shops.

"Gary!" Greg shouted.

"He's dead! Now move!"

Greg pulled his new gun by reflex as Welles pushed him toward the alley.

A dark figure leaped over the hood of the car, reminding Greg absurdly of some huge, malevolent frog. Welles' nine-millimeter exploded twice, and the korrigan spun away into the shadows.

"Move!"

Greg and Julie stumbled into the alley, with Welles a step behind.

"Keep going!" Welles shouted. "There'll be a store open up ahead!"

A scuttling noise came from the shadowed bulk of a dumpster to Greg's left. His fingers somehow fumbled his gun into the right position. "Alan, something in there!" he shouted.

Welles slowed his run and swung his pistol to cover the dumpster. "I hear it! Keep going!"

The night erupted with sound and movement as a figure leaped from the dumpster. Welles fired once, then it was on him. Greg started back to help, and something under an abandoned car reached out and clamped a steel grip on his ankle, yanking it out from under him.

Greg yelled, a cry of surprise and terror that was cut off when he crashed to the broken asphalt. He lost the gun and groped for it, dimly aware of Julie's scream as a second set of claws clamped around his leg. He stopped fumbling for the gun and yanked the pepper spray container clipped to his belt. He pressed one finger down hard and held it there, aiming in the general direction of his feet as he kicked frantically. The pressure on his legs disappeared, and he scrambled away, one hand falling on the pistol and scooping it up.

As Greg got to his feet, eyes watering from the spray, he heard movement again and saw the korrigan's shape forming up for a leap as it crawled from under the car. Instinctively, he pointed the gun at it and fired twice. The creature staggered back against the vehicle, then turned and leaped away around the hood, trailing a leg.

Greg steadied himself and looked around. His legs and chest were hurting, and his heart kicking hard as he saw Welles was on the ground ten feet away, in a desperate struggle with another of the murderous creatures. Julie had found a board of some kind and brought it down with all her strength on the korrigan's back. There was a thud of impact and a hiss of breath as the korrigan swung at the makeshift club, tearing it out of Julie's hands.

"Shoot it!" she yelled.

"I can't!" He desperately tried to line up a shot against the squirming bodies so he wouldn't hit Welles. At that moment, Welles somehow got his pistol between his own body and the korrigan's. There was a muffled flash, and the detective shoved the thing off him. It scurried away as Greg and Julie reached Welles.

Greg grabbed Welles by the shoulder and helped him sit up. A sticky, hot wetness covered his hand.

"We've got to keep going!" Greg said.

Welles shook his head. One hand clutched his pistol, but the other was wrapped around his body.

"Greg!" Julie shouted.

Greg looked up. He could see movement in the faint glimmer of a streetlight at the mouth of the alley. At least five small, deadly shadowforms were moving cautiously up the alley, keeping to the sides, using cover, and slipping in and out of view. The nearest was maybe twenty yards away.

"Run!" Welles commanded.

"Not without you! Julie, get his other arm—"

"No!" Welles shook Greg's hand off. "Forget it, dammit! It tore my fucking guts out." Greg looked down to where Welles' hand was clamped over his stomach. He didn't look any closer.

"Run, damn it, both of you!" Welles said in a kind of weak shout. "Run—I'll keep them back." He sighted his pistol unsteadily down the alley. "Go!"

Greg released Welles. "Julie, go get help."

"Are you crazy?" Welles half turned, trying to point his gun at Greg. "I can hold 'em. Both of you go now, or you're dead!"

Greg glanced down the alley. The nearest shape was five steps away. There was a noise from above, and he jerked his head up. Something was moving on the roof of the two-story building next to them.

Welles fired at the nearest korrigan. "Go!" he screamed.

Desperate, sickened by what he was doing, Greg squeezed Welles' shoulder, released it again, and grabbed Julie's arm.

"Run!"

She fought his pull for a moment, trying to form words, then yielded.

They ran.

There were two more shots.

Greg glanced back, but all he saw was a writhing mass on the asphalt.

"Oh, God—" he heard. Julie was looking back, too.

"Don't look! Run!"

Something leaped from a rooftop and landed hard beside Greg. As it came down, a paw caught his left shoulder and knocked him sprawling. He lost the gun again, and he could hear a hiss of breathing and knew the thing was right on him. Suddenly, Julie was standing over him, and he heard the hiss and smelled the acrid fumes as she blasted pepper spray at the korrigan. Greg scrambled up, and he glimpsed the creature squirming on the ground as he grabbed Julie's hand, and they fled.

They came out of the north end of the alley at a dead run, wiping at their eyes, looking frantically for anything that might be open. A half-block down, on the far side of the street, shone the lighted sign of a liquor store.

"This way!" They pounded down the sidewalk. Greg was gasping for breath, and he could hear Julie doing the same. *How fast can a korrigan move? Short legs—but lots of power. Don't think! Run!*

They raced across the empty street. A single car was parked in front of the liquor store. The door sign said CLOSED, but Greg saw light and movement inside.

The two burst through the unlocked door, gasping with terror and the relief of finding sanctuary.

"Freeze, mother!"

Greg stared at the stocking-masked figure behind the counter.

The man held a pistol pointed at Greg's head. Greg's fear flooded a feeling of disbelief.

They had escaped into a hold-up.

20

J ulie and Greg were shoved to the floor next to the store clerk, a heavyset Black man who was shaking with terror.

"Wallets!" one gunman demanded, in a voice that betrayed some version of a Latino accent. Greg dug his from his pocket. He looked into the wavering muzzle of the man's revolver and was surprised he didn't feel more fear than he did. Maybe his emotions were just overloaded.

"Listen. Nobody talks, and nobody calls cops. Understand?"

The three victims nodded in unison. The man ripped the cord from the back of the store's wall phone and scooped the clerk's cell off the counter. "You sit tight, and you live."

The two started edging toward the door, keeping their guns on the victims.

"Don't go out there!" Julie cried.

The two stared at her. "What you say, bitch?" the taller one asked.

"I said, don't go out there. You'll get killed!"

"You tellin' me what? Bangers? Five-O?"

"No, not gang members or cops. It's—" her voice trailed off.

The man who'd spoken laughed. "You weird, bitch. Want me to stay and play with you? Love to, but no time. 'Bye now."

The gunmen left, the bell tied to the shop's front door tinkling behind them.

Julie shook her head weakly. "Oh, God," she moaned.

Greg squeezed her hand. "It's okay. We're okay. Why'd you try to stop them?"

"They must be right outside!"

The store clerk began to move, sliding away from them as if he feared them, too. "What the hell you two talkin' about?"

"You wouldn't believe us," Greg said grimly. "Are you okay?"

"Will be, soon as I quit my job. I got another phone in the back. I'm calling the cops, and then I'm outta here. I don't work for this place anymore."

The man gained his feet and hurried toward the back office.

Greg helped Julie up, feeling the shaking she was fighting to suppress. They clung to each other, Greg leaning against a display case of chilled beer. The adrenaline wave broke, making his body shake and his eyes squeeze shut for a long minute until it receded. He looked around, but they were still alone. He was becoming aware of his scrapes and developing bruises, and they hurt. Julie seemed to have gotten off more lightly.

"What now?" she asked.

"We wait for the cops," he said. "We've got no money, no ID, no phones, and no gun. We'll have to ask the cops to call Billings—he's the only one who knows us."

"The only one left. God, what an awful way to die." Julie slumped into his arms, so exhausted she was limp.

"I know how you feel, but we're not going to be able to rest for a long time," Greg said. "We need to be able to give statements and take the cops back over the scene."

He reached up into a cooler and took out a bottle of Sprite. "Remind me to pay the guy for this." He took an aspirin box from his pocket and extracted two pink pills. He tossed one into his mouth, washed it down with the soda, and then handed the other pill to Julie.

"What's that?"

"Cafergot. Like a half-dozen cups of coffee. It'll keep you awake."

"Don't want to be awake," she muttered, but she took the drug. Then she buried her head in his chest, and they waited for the cops.

* * *

In a small conference room at the Southwest Division station, Billings glared at them—not a genuinely hostile expression, Greg thought, but the look of an angry man who didn't know what to do or who to be angry at. He glanced at the signed printouts of their statements and shook his head.

"Mr. Preston, we have three dead officers," he declared. "One maybe murdered, two for sure. And we've got your two stiffs who robbed this place lying in the middle of the street with masks and guns. They never even got off a shot. Your goddam little elves have been busy, or so you'll probably tell me."

"Look at the bodies, Lieutenant," Greg said wearily. He felt his bruised appendages stiffening up, and it made him even less patient. "Try to tell me it was done with knives, or attack dogs, or whatever. You know better."

"Yes, I know better!" Billings was standing across a dark wooden table from Greg and Julie, and he slammed a hand down on the tabletop. "And you're sitting here so smug and happy because you made morons out of us."

Greg rose. "That is enough, Lieutenant." He spat out the title. "Do we look happy to you? Don't you think I wish to God I'd been totally wrong?"

"No, I don't think so! You write about this kind of shit, and you finally got some proof some of it's real! You're thrilled, aren't you!"

Greg stared in genuine disbelief. "And you're insane. My best friend, your cops, God knows how many other people dead, these things trying to kill both of us, and you think I'm happy about it." He trembled with rage. "No, I'm not, and I don't think you're that nuts! I think you're furious with yourself for having your head up your ass and refusing to admit this was happening. Now you're trying to blame me somehow! Well, listen—"

"Stop it!" Julie leaped up, her eyes blazing. "You've both lost it and guess what—it's not going to help one damn bit!"

Billings started to speak, but she glared at him so fiercely he choked off his words.

"Now, none of this is going to do any good," she said, her voice low but commanding. "There are dead people, including a man I loved, and there are going to be lots more, including Greg and me, if we don't stop it. Now, can we please talk about that?"

Billings appeared to waver, then nodded. "All right." He put his hands up as if in surrender. "You're right. Whether it's everybody's fault or nobody's fault doesn't matter right now. Let's sit back down here and decide what the hell to do."

They all sat. A uniformed cop from Southwest popped his head in and asked if anybody wanted anything. Julie asked for tea, but they didn't have it, so the visitors made do with coffee.

"All right," Billings said. His dark brown eyes were still alive with frustration and fury, but the atmosphere of imminent hostility had evaporated. "Preston, what would you do if you were me?"

Coming from the acerbic lieutenant, the question surprised Greg, and he had to think for a moment.

"These things aren't human," he said finally. "But it's like I told Welles. They've acted pretty much like primitive humans—maybe humans with a warrior mindset—would do in this situation. All they can think of to do is kill anyone who knows about them. I don't know what their plans are for the longer term. They probably don't even have any.

"When it comes to targeting other people, I don't know if they only kill people who they see with us or if they can detect traces of our scent on people we've been around. Losing Captain Lear made this a lot scarier for a lot more people. I guess you and Dr. Sporkin are very likely victims."

"You haven't answered my question yet."

Greg leaned back, closing his eyes. It was the first time all day he'd felt safe enough to do so. Despite the surge from the cafergot, he felt sleep lurking behind his eyes like some shadowy thing, but he didn't want to give in to it. He knew it would hold dreams about the horror they'd just witnessed.

He opened his eyes. "We've got to draw them out, Lieutenant. You can hunt them all over town, but you'll never find them. They have to be lured in."

"Greg, I don't like what you're leading up to again," Julie said.

"I like it even less." In fact, just thinking about it scared him down to his soul. But it was a distant kind of fear as if dulled by the carnage he'd seen.

"There's no other way, Lieutenant. We have to offer bait that's so attractive they'll come after it without thinking to be careful. Only Julie or I would be that attractive to them. It sure as hell isn't going to be her, so I guess that leaves me."

"No!" Julie said. "Greg, I just lost one man I cared about. Now you're going to get yourself killed, too?"

"Julie, if I don't do this, I get killed sooner or later. We both do. We can't watch our steps every minute without slipping up and giving them an opening. And we can't just run away and let them keep slaughtering people who have no idea what's happening. And they can't evacuate L.A. and nuke it, either. What options does that leave us?"

Julie closed her eyes as she spoke. "Of all the time I've known you, why did you have to pick now to be right?"

"I always had a rotten sense of timing. Besides, if we do this right, we all live and get to try to rebuild something like normal lives."

"That's hardly guaranteed," she said. Her voice held a quiet tremor.

"Nothing is, especially not now. Don't think I'm out to be some kind of macho guy. I've never been so scared. I just don't see anything else I can do."

Billings cleared his throat. "Let's put this on hold for the moment. I'll get Dr. Sporkin back in the morning, but even before that I'll be talking to all the brass we woke up when we found out we had officers killed. You two look too burned out to even think straight. I'll find you a safe place to rack out. By the way, we have your wallet from that robber and your purse from the car. Umm...do you think you need a sleeping pill or something? You've been through an awful lot."

Greg eyed the lieutenant's face again. His compassion seemed sincere, and he had a determined expression in place of the unfocused anger he'd had before. Maybe the self-centered bureaucrat Welles described had, in the face of the crisis, been banished, and the real cop Billings must have once been was surfacing again.

Julie shook her head. "I think I'm going to have a good cry," she said to Greg. "It's been a long time since I did that, but I'm sure as hell going to do it now."

"I could use some ibuprofen or something," he said. "I didn't get any real puncture wounds from claws, but my ankle and shoulder hurt pretty good."

"You want a doctor?"

"No, I'm ok. Just something to take the edge off."

"No problem."

Greg edged as close to Julie as he could without falling off his chair. He looked back at Billings.

"There's one other thing, though. They took a shot at us and missed. They're going to be in a really rotten mood. Like I said, Sporkin's in danger."

"I'll take care of him," Billings said crisply. "We'll guard him while he does the autopsies, then bring him in with us."

"Guard him damn good, then. They probably don't like the risks of breaking into buildings, but they'll do it when they have to."

"So I've seen. Look, I'll ask the guys here if you can use their cot room to get some rest. As for me, you'll have to excuse me." His voice became quiet. "I have to go wake up a cop's wife and tell her her husband is dead."

21

Greg and Julie passed the night on two cots that had been stuck in a small room for cops too busy to go home. They pushed the cots together and slumped down on them immediately. Billings, continuing to show his surprising streak of humanity, had found time to send a car to bring their bags from Fernandez's apartment.

Greg closed the door to the mini-bunkroom and Julie curled up next to him for the cry she'd promised herself. He had a bit of one, too.

Julie fell asleep first. Greg watched her, barely able to discern her outline in the crack of light that came under the door. He'd never experienced such a nonstop onslaught of emergency, crisis, and disaster. No one had ever tried to kill him. Yet they'd lived when armed cops had dies. So weird.

After commanding a tank in Afghanistan, Toby Williamson told him combat was a test with no grades—it was pass or fail. If you were alive, you passed. What Welles had said was pretty similar. So he had a passing grade so far—he and Julie were both surviving, having saved each other's necks at least once apiece. There was no point in keeping score.

From that thought, his brain jumped onto the track he'd been trying to avoid thinking about—the feelings between himself and Julie. He was utterly unable to sort them out in any way that made sense.

So, do I love her? Always have. Does she love me? She said she did, but hell, how can she know what she thinks right now?

With a supreme effort, Greg gave up thinking and just held her. His exhaustion finally overruled everything else, and he, too, was asleep.

* * *

Greg awoke, according to his watch, at 7:32 the next morning. Monday morning, he thought. The start of a new week.

Leaving Julie to sleep, he opened the door and poked his head out.

"Oh, Mr. Preston," a voice immediately called. Greg turned, startled. A two-stripe patrol officer, an Asian guy who looked too young to wear a uniform, was sitting on a chair in the hall, obviously on guard.

"Hi," Greg said.

"I'm Officer Fong. Lieutenant Billings posted me to keep an eye on you. He was very concerned that you not step outside the station without an escort."

"Thanks. He say anything else?"

"He wants me to escort you to a meeting downtown at zero nine hundred. You've got time if you want to shower. We have locker rooms here and stuff."

"I would love that."

"I'll have one of the women officers show your friend around."

"Thanks."

* * *

At ten till nine, they were being escorted into the PAB. Fong talked briefly to the cop at the desk.

"You guys are wanted upstairs," he told them. "Like way up, in the OCP boardroom. Tenth floor."

Billings met them when they got off the elevator. "Ready?" he asked.

"I guess," Greg said. "Who else is here?"

"The big shots." Billings led them through a four-desk anteroom, where they received some curious looks, and to a well-appointed conference space with expensive chairs, an expansive view of downtown, and a highly polished granite or fake-granite conference table.

While he was still in the doorway, Billings half-turned and pointed out the people in the room. All were standing in a tight group, talking so earnestly they hadn't noticed the newcomers.

"That's Assistant Chief Henderson from Operations," he whispered, pointing out a slightly paunchy, gray-haired Black cop with soft, rounded features and wire-rimmed glasses. "You know Dr. Sporkin. Captain Eric Ryzinsky is the Homicide Special Section chief and is acting head of RHD. That's Lieutenant Diaz. He heads up D Platoon—SWAT. Oh, and that guy is a Mr. Creighton from the mayor's office."

"Damn," Greg said quietly.

Billings grinned for the first time since Greg had met him. "I know what you mean. Speaking of which, don't underestimate Henderson because he looks like a teddy bear. He had to let Creighton in but swung a lot of weight to keep out twenty other brass and politicians for now. The news of officers being killed gets everyone hopped up real quick."

Now Henderson noticed the visitors and waved them in. Billings introduced Greg and Julie, and Henderson nodded toward open seats. Everyone sat down except the Assistant Chief.

"Well, let's get down to business," Henderson said. "Lieutenant Billings, an overview of the case up to now, please."

"Yes, sir." Billings looked at some notes in his hand, then stood up and pointed at the site of last night's attack on a city map on a big monitor behind him.

He sketched the facts quickly and, to Greg's relief, open-mindedly.

As he went, he mentioned the various theories that had been formulated and discarded.

"Last night, of course, you all know about," he continued. "An ambush where two detectives died. The fact of the murders has leaked to the press. The circumstances we have so far managed to keep to ourselves. The officers from Southwest acted commendably in putting up a wide perimeter immediately and keeping people out."

"Very good, Lieutenant," Henderson said. "Now comes the part I'm still trying to get my brain around. Dr. Sporkin, would you take over?"

Sporkin stepped up to a podium.

"Detective Fernandez was killed in his car," he announced. "Something broke through the window from outside. The cause of death was sharp force injuries to the throat, apparently inflicted by a clawed animal's paw or hand."

Greg looked around for reactions. The cops showed none so far. Creighton, a tall, thin white guy with large ears and reddish hair, was biting his lip hard.

"The second officer, Detective Welles, died approximately sixty feet away. He showed only minor injuries from the crash. Cause of death: sharp force injuries to the abdomen, throat, and chest."

Julie choked off a tiny sound. Greg squeezed her hand.

"Neither body displayed the unusual bone puncture wounds found in the previous fatalities we believe are related. I can go into detail if you like."

"No, thank you," Henderson said.

"I have only one question at this point," Henderson said. "Are we —beyond any doubt—dealing with animals, or could we be dealing with some kind of deranged killers who dress and act like animals?"

"Chief, there is no such possibility," Dr. Sporkin said. "I found this extremely hard to believe. Actually, that's an understatement. This seemed like science fiction. Fantasy. Impossible. Ridiculous. Pick any word you want.

"However, I do believe what shows up in my microscopes and the serology tests. I'd stake my entire reputation—and, in fact, I'm doing exactly that—that we are dealing with a bizarre and totally unknown predator species. Whatever it is, and however it happened that it first turned up in Los Angeles, California, it's here. We have to deal with that."

"All right," Henderson said, shaking his head. "I guess I have to believe you, but for God's sake, this doesn't go outside this room to anyone not personally cleared by me. We're staking the entire Department's reputation on this, too.

"Here's the second part I don't like," Henderson added. "It is absolutely against Department policy to allow a civilian to be used as a decoy to lure dangerous criminals. However, Lieutenant Billings and Dr. Sporkin have convinced me we may have to do something like that to prevent many more killings. I wanted to put an officer in your clothes as the lure, but Dr. Sporkin thinks the things' sense of smell is so good they'd detect the difference. So, Mr. Preston, are you sure about volunteering here?"

Greg's voice sounded distant like he was listening to someone else. "Yes, sir."

"Do you think they'll fall for it?"

"Chief, there's something strange about these things. They're intelligent and organized, but they have a blind spot. Once they decide someone or something is a threat, they keep coming after it, even when it would be smarter to break off. They're going to come. I know they are."

"All right. Lieutenant Diaz, you've been working out the plan."

"Yes, sir, I have." Diaz was an athletic-looking Hispanic with heavy, dark eyebrows over black eyes that still betrayed some doubt. "On the assumption, of course, that little dwarf monsters have in fact invaded Los Angeles."

Greg started to stand, but Julie grabbed his arm, and Dr. Sporkin answered for him.

"Lieutenant, doubt in this matter is understandable but irrelevant. If we had time, I could take you to the lab and show you, but I guarantee these wounds were not inflicted by a metal blade or by any animal known. To expand on that, it bears repeating that we are dealing with a creature of unknown species and origin. Tissue samples show a cell structure unlike any terrestrial creature, living or extinct. A creature, I may add, that has been hit by nine-millimeter bullets and shotgun pellets and taken an eight-story fall without lethal effects. Those are the facts, Lieutenant, whether we like them or not."

"Let's go on," Henderson growled.

"Yes, sir," Diaz said. "Assuming this is all correct, then, we do think we have a plan. Dave, some of my people, and I got up very early this morning and put this together."

A laptop-driven projector came on, and Diaz gestured to image on an old-fashioned portable screen. "This is the floor diagram of a small warehouse on Eighth Street. The owners were arrested for trafficking, and the building was locked up. I have men in there now clearing the floor space.

"As you can see, the first floor is an almost unobstructed single room. There's a small office area built onto the north end. That contains the only ground-floor windows.

"With that office area closed up, there are only two entrances— these loading doors on the east side and this one in the west wall. There is a stairway and a freight elevator to the second floor on the south end, right here." Diaz looked around, apparently for a pointer, scowled and tapped the screen with his finger to indicate the stairs.

"The lure—if you'll pardon the wording, Mr. Preston—will be here, near the base of the stairs. The office entrance and the east doors will be secured, leaving only the single loading door on the west side.

"The 'creatures' will enter that door. As soon as they do, Mr. Preston will retreat to the second floor. At the top of the stairwell will be three SWAT teams. Others will be in vans outside, in position to move and block the west door behind the subjects. The first-floor lights will then be switched on—we'll rig a master switch at the top of the stairs—and the creatures will be taken out."

Diaz paused for the first time, standing at parade rest while the others contemplated the plan.

"This is unreal," Creighton muttered. "The city of Los Angeles is building a monster trap."

"I have as hard a time comprehending it as you do, Will," Henderson said. "But I can't get away from it. My men are dead, and all the evidence says this is what's happening."

"Mr. Preston, you're the expert, I hear," Diaz said. "What do you think?" Greg thought he still detected an undertone of challenge in the man's voice.

"I don't see any holes in it," Greg said. "Except maybe you're betting the korrigans won't smell—literally smell—your trap."

"Just how well do they smell?" The question came from the hitherto-silent Captain Ryzinsky.

Ryzinsky was a compact fellow who, at an age Greg guessed at forty-five, still had obvious weightlifting muscles showing through the ever-present white shirt.

"As well as a wolf or a bloodhound," Greg said. "They'll know there's other people, and I'd bet they know the smell of guns by now. It might help to put some kind of covering over whatever type of door or opening is at the top of those stairs. Just a thin plastic sheet might do. Maybe that way, it'll smell to them like I'm more isolated from you. And keep the vans outside a block away."

"I can't believe you're discussing this so calmly," Julie said, the strain audible in her voice. "This is your life, Greg. I won't make you quote Gary Cooper or somebody, but if you do this, you have to be absolutely certain it will work, and you won't get yourself killed."

Greg nodded in what he hoped was a reassuring way. "Julie, we are at risk everywhere right now. Probably even in this room. As to why I'm discussing this calmly, I'm a good actor. Inside, I'm halfway to the airport."

There were a few chuckles from around the room. Then Henderson took over again. "Mr. Preston, I salute your courage. You do not have to do this."

"There isn't another option," Greg said. "I'll do it."

The Assistant Chief nodded. "All right. Captain Ryzinsky, you're the operational head of the task force under my supervision. Lieutenants Billings and Diaz are assigned to you for the duration. Pull anyone from SWAT, RHD, Metro, or anywhere else you need. If you need any specialized equipment from Anti-Terrorism, I'll clear it. This has to be done as fast as possible, or else the news will get out, and it will make the panic over the I-5 Killer look like nothing at all."

Diaz nodded and turned to the medical examiner. "Dr. Sporkin, anything you can add about how to kill these things? Where it's best to shoot them, anything like that?"

Sporkin rubbed his chin. "Where, I can't say for sure. I assume their anatomy is at least a little like ours, so a headshot is best. I will tell you not to worry about wasting bullets. Hit them as many times as you can. What worries me is that your men might have to be at very close range before the bullets will have the desired effects."

"They're quick—damn quick," Greg interjected. "Headshots might not be possible. A shotgun seemed to work pretty good."

"We'll have the full SWAT arsenal ready, Mr. Preston," Diaz said. "If they're as sensitive to daylight as you say they are, we'll throw some flash-bang grenades in first. Those should stun them and make them easier targets."

"I think you're correct," Sporkin said.

Greg nodded and turned to Diaz. "How do we keep the flash bangs from blinding us?"

"My men will have goggles," Diaz said. "You'll be on the second floor, out of the way."

"I want the goggles," Greg said. "If the timing's a little off, I don't want to be a blind duck as well as a sitting one. I want the gun Welles gave me back, too."

Diaz looked doubtful. "We're going to have to discuss that."

"I figured you'd say that."

22

When Diaz said "arsenal," Greg thought, he wasn't kidding.

Greg looked around. He hadn't known a police force, even in a large city in a world of terrorism and drug lords, really possessed an armory like you saw on TV. The walls of the SWAT armory were almost completely hidden by racks and shelves filled with weapons, including submachine guns, assault rifles, carbines, and countless red and olive-drab ammunition boxes. A broad-shouldered, sandy-haired man in civilian clothes was conversing with Lt. Diaz, explaining something about what looked like an automatic shotgun.

"It's like an Army base in here," Julie said, obviously impressed.

"Well, I, for one, am glad to see it," Greg said. "I think we're going to need everything they've got."

Diaz turned to Greg and Julie. "I brought you here to make your minds a little easier," he said. "These things are apparently pretty tough, but I don't think they're tougher than the drug soldiers this unit takes on all the time."

"Maybe not tougher, but different," Greg said. "If you tell your guys anything, it's to remind them these things are not human. They may not think like people and probably won't react like people. Your men have to be ready for anything they do."

"Understood," Diaz said. "Sergeant Christopher?"

The armorer in civvies came over and was introduced. "Okay, so you're the guy our targets will be after," he said to Greg.

"That's me."

"Okay. Let's see if we can even up the odds. I understand you've got some experience with a semi-automatic pistol?"

"Yes. Including one time last night for real."

"We'll try to get you more practice if there's time." The sergeant's large, constantly busy hands produced a heavy black matte-finished semi-automatic with the slide locked open. With it went a black fabric holster. "Lieutenant Diaz asked us to give you more stopping power, so this is a Kimber Custom Two forty-five ACP. Everyone in SWAT carries them. Think you can handle it?"

"Yeah."

Christopher handed him a magazine. "Eight rounds. Clearing barrel's over there. Load it so you can get the feel."

Greg slid a magazine in, worked the slide, engaged the thumb safety, unloaded it, and repeated the cycle. "I'm good," he said.

Christopher gave Greg a slightly puzzled look. "The lieutenant told me you're going with the platoon chasing some kind of dangerous animal, but he won't tell me what. That right?"

"Some kind," Greg said.

"Okay." The armorer glanced at Diaz. "Apparently, *somebody* here thinks the details are above my pay grade, but I can still help you. What do these animals weigh?"

"Well, they're short but awfully well-muscled—dense, I guess you'd say. Maybe ninety pounds."

"Like a big baboon?"

"A lot like that, really."

"Then, no problem. The forty-five will knock a ninety-pound target into next week." He produced a belt pouch. "Two more magazines in there. Do you want a vest?"

"Sounds good to me."

Christopher opened a gray metal cabinet and produced a heavy-looking garment.

"This isn't the usual armor for stopping bullets. Since you're dealing with claws, I'm giving you the vest guards use at the jail. It's stab-resistant. Should be teeth-resistant and claw-resistant, too. "

"Should be?" Greg asked.

"Well, we can't say for certain unless we get someone to jump in the lion cage at the zoo, but trust me. It's *very* resistant."

Greg strapped the vest on with help from the sergeant. He moved around a little, adjusted it, and nodded. "That's not bad. It doesn't slow me up too much."

Julie thumped her hand on the vest. "I hope it works as well as you say."

"Ma'am, to me, all the boys who go out in the field on this team are my responsibility. I don't lose them."

"Thanks. That's good to know. But I'd also like to know more about how the officers will protect him."

Diaz said, "I'll cover that in the tactical briefing. Come on in and listen."

* * *

They slid into chairs at the back of the spacious modern briefing room. It was filled with SWAT officers, all wearing dark blue Nomex combat suits. Greg had expected a SWAT team to look like an NFL linebacking corps, but there were little wiry guys, big broad ones, and even a blond woman who reminded him fleetingly of Karen Montrose.

Diaz, already wearing a standard SWAT black balaclava and carrying a black "Fritz" helmet with a built-in radio, walked briskly to the podium and signaled for silence.

"I know some of you guys are wondering what the hell we're doing," he began bluntly. "I was, too, but what it comes down to is that we don't have the luxury of stopping to think about it. We're dealing with animals. Animals more dangerous than anything you ever heard of.

"Whatever jungle hideout or whatever bad science fiction movie these things came out of, they are real, and they are killing people in our city, and we have to kill them. Any question on that?"

There were no questions.

"This is not a pushover," Diaz said. "If you think it is because the targets are unarmed, we've got dead officers who would disagree with you. Think of these things as tigers or lions. If experience is any guide, you may have to shoot them to pieces to stop them.

"That's why we have assembled the entire SWAT force for this deployment, plus twenty backup officers from Metro and other divisions. We'll need the heaviest firepower we can throw. For those joining us for this mission, everyone has the MP5 submachine gun or the Benilli twelve-gauge shotgun. Double aught buck for the shotguns. Three-round burst for the MP5s. We've picked out three rooftops for the observers and snipers. They'll be up there to give us warning and pick off targets trying to escape."

"Let me add something there," Ryzinsky said. "This may be our only chance to get them all together—and let me remind you, we do not know how many there are. We have to try to get every one of them, whether there are six or a hundred. We think there are only a few because otherwise, we'd have had many more killings so far. But if we are outmatched—just in case there are more of these things than we think—Lieutenant Diaz will give the abort command, and everyone will pull out immediately. Do NOT try to be a hero. I'll be a couple of blocks away with the BEAR as a mobile command post. Two RAs with ER docs will be with us in case of casualties. SID Field Investigation is on alert to move in quickly to see what they can learn. Hopefully, they'll just have bodies to study."

Diaz took over again. "Now, our own experts and our civilian consultants, who have seen more of these things than anyone else, have some important advice. On the good side, these things hate the light, so flash bangs should really freak them out. On the bad, they can jump like kangaroos, so be ready. That increases the dangers of fratricide. No matter what happens, you watch for other officers."

He turned to a wall chart showing the warehouse. "We're already clearing out the surrounding area on the pretense of hunting for some really nasty drug dealers. The plan is to be in place by 2100. All the entrances are sealed except this one door. Three elements concealed on the second floor, one in the offices. All stay in cover until the targets enter the building. Backup units from Rampart Division surrounding the perimeter."

He described their preparations as Greg and Julie tried to memorize every detail. From what Greg knew of police and military tactics —which, he admitted to himself, was not a lot—this seemed a well-planned undertaking. The bizarre, unbelievable nature of the whole situation hadn't deterred the SWAT commanders from a thorough and professional approach to the operation.

Then it was time to go.

* * *

Everything was in place.

Greg paced in the emptiness of the warehouse. He hated the openness of the first floor—the way it made his quiet footsteps echo and shadows seemed to move. The space was maybe sixty feet by a hundred, but it loomed larger in the dimness.

Greg was already tired. He'd insisted on walking most of the way here, determined to leave an unambiguous scent trail toward the warehouse—and away from Julie. He thought of her last words to him, a whispered, "Stay safe." She was with Henderson now in something called the EOC, which supposedly was completely secure.

Greg nervously clutched the pistol in his right hand. They'd gotten in some practice shooting, and he'd done well for being rusty and nervous. The tennis reflexes and muscles helped, he figured.

He left the firing range with an official laminated CCW permit for the SWAT .45. Diaz and Henderson let Greg carry the gun for this event only when he insisted. After drilling into him, they relented that he must not, under any circumstances, be the first person to fire, or fire at all except in self-defense. Let the cops judge the moment to shoot.

If all went well, he would have no need to do any shooting himself. If the korrigans followed the script. Greg pushed his goggles up a little higher on his forehead and looked at the shadows again. He did his 3-D visualization trick, picturing the outlines of the warehouse. There were several ways to approach the loading door, but the way the cops had arranged things, no other way in. He'd see them when they used that door.

There was a creaking sound behind him as Sergeant Dave Meyer shifted position. Meyer, one of Diaz's most experienced SWAT officers, was crouched at the foot of the stairs. The husky, round-faced cop had been designated Greg's bodyguard and was waiting, shotgun in his hands, to cover Greg's retreat.

Meyer scuttled a little closer, and Greg turned his head.

Meyer silently mouthed the word *coming*. He pointed at the loading door.

Greg nodded. One of the snipers, he guessed, had spotted something.

Then Greg heard a sound beside his heart. It was barely there, a whispered echo across the warehouse, a quiet scraping. What scraping on what? He raised the gun, squinting toward the loading door. Damn, he was sweating a lot.

Movement?

Something dark. Tiny. Below the loading door. A rat.

No. Not a rat. A hand. Or whatever the hell you called it.

Greg slid his feet backward, deliberately digging in his Wilson Crossfire tennis shoes to make little squeaks on the concrete floor.

"Dave!" he whispered harshly. "Here they come!"

Meyer rose, bringing his gun up and talking quietly into his helmet mike.

"Get back here," the officer hissed.

"I've got to wait just a second," Greg insisted, shooting down the voice in his head that agreed with Meyer. He clutched his pistol tighter. Suddenly, he felt suffocated by his vest.

The first korrigan became visible. It put one hand on the floor in ape fashion, keeping low, scuttling over the exposed threshold like a giant spider. In a moment, it had blended into the shadows just inside the loading door.

Greg waited, a few more endless heartbeats.

There was no more movement. *They're cautious*, Greg thought. *They smell it. If I don't do this just right, I won't lure them in.*

He made a quick, panicky-looking turn toward the stairs. He tripped himself and feigned a cry of pain as he fell.

"No," he snapped to Meyer, who was already moving to aid him. "It's an act!" At least the things didn't understand English. He tried to rise and fell down again, trying to look as injured as he could.

There was movement behind him.

"Greg, come on!"

As Meyer sprang toward him, Greg glanced over his shoulder. Another spider-shape, then more of them. Meyer grabbed his arm, and they staggered toward the stairs, Greg still acting hurt.

Still more sounds, too many sounds. The korrigans bought it, all right. If the things could smell fear, Greg thought, he didn't have to fake that.

The sounds were right behind him.

"Go!" Meyer yelled, shoving him. Greg raced for the stairs, grabbed the railing, and turned around as Meyer's first shotgun blast exploded.

The gun boomed again, and cops were storming down the steps, shoving Greg aside. There was a commotion near the loading door, cops flooding in, the door starting to roll down.

WHAM!

The goggles—

Greg yanked his goggles down over his now-sightless eyes as pain lanced through his skull from his eyes and ears. He lost his balance, stumbled for real this time, and crashed into an awkward sitting position on the steps. Gunfire crashed—the explosion of shotguns, the ripping staccato of the submachine guns. Greg began crawling half-sideways up the steps, one hand still clutching the pistol as shouts and thunder and dimly seen lightning burst around him.

He reached a landing and paused, trying to get his mind and body in some sort of order as the tumult continued. He flinched as a stray bullet knocked splinters from the wooden railing. Sight began to come back, slowly, like dawn trying to break through an overcast sky, although he could tell the first floor was flooded with light.

Greg saw shapes running, dodging and crying out and shooting. There were smaller shapes, too, moving in leaps and bursts, and some of both the small and the large shapes were not moving at all but only lying on the floor.

Grasping the railing again, Greg pulled himself up, watching with clearing vision but pounding head as the hellish game-to-the-death continued. The korrigans seemed caught between the imperatives to attack and to escape, the cops spinning and twisting as they tried for clear shots. A korrigan made a great leap between two men, and Greg felt a staggering wave of nausea as one cop fired his shotgun an instant late and caught his partner too high for the vest, and the pellets tore into his throat. One korrigan tried to climb the exposed studs of the walls, but that made it an easy target, and it fell away in a hail of bullets. The rest kept dodging or counterattacked with fierce desperation, springing for the throats of the men even as bullets thudded into them.

The tide was turning toward the police. A door opened from the office area, and two more five-man SWAT elements poured through. One by one, the korrigans were hurled to the floor by the incessant crossfire.

Two leaped straight for the stairs.

Greg crouched, fell back, shouted, and fired all at once, and the korrigans bounded over and past him and through the torn plastic to the second floor.

A cop ran after them, shotgun swinging in one hand as he charged up the stairs.

"Don't go up there alone!" Greg yelled. Desperately, he raised his own weapon and raced after the officer.

He found the body just at the top of the stairs. The man had no face. Fighting another surge of nausea, Greg looked around in the poor light cast by a few overhead bulbs. Twenty feet away, two figures scrambled over some crates toward a many-paned window.

"Stop!" Greg yelled ridiculously. One korrigan reached the window and halted a moment, pushing at it, silhouetted in the dim light against the painted-over glass.

Greg fired.

The slug hit the creature in the back, driving it through the window in a crash of glass fragments and splintered wooden mullions. The second korrigan leaped after it.

Greg raced to the window and looked out, leaning on a crate and gasping for breath as he searched the street below. He heard one shot, apparently from one of the rooftop snipers, followed by a crack as the bullet hit the pavement. Then, one more shot, hitting something else, not a ricochet. That was it—if the cops had had a target, they'd lost it.

The streetlight glow splashed over the pavement showed nothing but the window debris. No korrigans, living or dead, were visible.

On the first floor, Greg found the aftermath of a war. Cops were kneeling over dead or wounded officers while other cops poked with their gun barrels at dead korrigans. No one spoke except for words of comfort to the injured and the latter's moans of pain. Policemen, hardened veterans of the urban battle zone, many of them veterans of war as well, looked at the carnage with disbelieving eyes. The smell was something Greg couldn't find anything to compare to.

Julie kept calling it a nightmare, Greg remembered. It wasn't. It was infinitely worse. He tried not to look at the blood and bodies strewn about the warehouse. From outside came the wailing sirens of ambulances.

"Diaz!" Greg's own shout made his ears ring. "Lieutenant Diaz!"

Diaz looked up from Greg's left, where he was crouched over a twitching, blood-splattered figure that ten minutes ago had been one of his men.

"Over here," Diaz said without rising.

Greg knelt beside him. Diaz turned, and Greg saw he was holding his right hand to the side of his face. Blood seeped between his fingers. His radio helmet had been knocked off, and it lay on the floor a few feet away.

Diaz read Greg's face. "Yeah, me, too," he said through gritting teeth. "You happy with your monster hunt?"

"It's not over," Greg said, reluctantly but urgently.

Diaz stared at him.

"Two dove through an upstairs window. Well, one did. The other fell through when I shot it. I heard two shots from sniper rifles."

"Shit," Diaz said passionately. "Sergeant Meyer, take two teams and sweep the area. Two got out—at least one wounded! Find 'em!"

Meyer looked dismayed, then nodded and headed off at a run, waving other men to follow.

Diaz glanced up at Greg again. "Any chance they'll find them?"

"Pretty slim. May have gone down a sewer or something by now."

A moment later, the paramedics came in, stethoscopes and bandage scissors dangling off their dark blue uniform shirts. The first one to enter through the reopened loading door was a youngster who took one look, froze for a moment, then ripped off his surgical mask and shoved his partner aside in his haste to bolt outside and throw up.

Lieutenant Diaz looked at the officer killed by friendly fire. "God damn it," he said. "In the whole history of SWAT, no one ever got killed by another cop who lost discipline. *Ever*." He looked over toward the nearest wall, where the cop who had fired the fatal shot was retching onto the floor. A couple of his colleagues were hovering around him but not touching him, not saying anything, probably having no idea what to say.

Diaz turned back to Greg. "These monsters freak everybody out, and we've still got more of them? Preston, can these things breed?"

"We've no idea how they do it," Greg said, "but they have to reproduce somehow."

"Shit," Diaz said again.

* * *

The paramedics and ambulance crews had recovered from their initial shock and were now hard at work. An EMS Captain, an Asian woman named Nguyen who radiated a take-no-prisoners attitude, was rapidly moving from patient to patient, giving brief, urgent directions to the others.

Diaz, with Greg in tow, went up to the captain. "How are they?"

"Counting four dead, nine seriously injured," the captain said. She glanced at Diaz's face and pulled away the lieutenant's hand to examine the injury more closely. "That looks like it needs stitches," she said. "Nely!" she called. "Fix up the lieutenant."

A slender Hispanic paramedic promptly tried to collar Diaz, but he waved them off. "I'll live," he said. "Take care of my men."

"We are," Nguyen said, nodding to where the ambulance crews had already scooped up at least two cops. "At least let them clean that up and get a bandage on it. Now, what the hell are those things?" She pointed at a dead korrigan.

"Martians," Diaz snapped. "Get back to my people." She shot him a glare but hustled off. Diaz turned to the nearest officer. "Get tarps or body bags over these things *now*," he said. "We don't need any more people seeing what they are."

"'Martian' was as good an answer as any," Greg told him. "Might even be right. What now?"

Diaz again shooed away the still-hovering paramedic and pointed at the door to the office area. "Now it hits the fan."

Greg looked. Assistant Chief Henderson, with Ryzinsky, Sporkin, and Creighton. had arrived. They emerged slowly, looking around with dazed expressions.

"Lieutenant Diaz!" Henderson spotted the SWAT commander and charged over. "What the hell happened here?"

"Isn't it pretty obvious, sir?"

Henderson looked around again and shook his head.

Sporkin went to help with the injured. Ryzinsky stayed close behind the Assistant Chief, and Creighton swayed a little and grabbed the stair rail for support.

"Dear God," Henderson said. "They're real. There really are things like this."

"I've been telling you that," Greg said. "And, as I told Lieutenant Diaz, there are two live ones left. That's assuming they all were here tonight, of course." He had already counted the dead korrigans. There were seven. The cops, out of caution or rage, had made sure there were no live ones left in the building.

"Two got out?" Henderson asked.

"I've got men out looking for them," Diaz said. "Mr. Preston hit one with a forty-five, and Winkler on the roof says she nailed one with a round but saw it bounce right back up. Don't know if they both hit the same one, but we need to push out the perimeter. We have to hunt the damn things down."

Henderson nodded. "Let's work on that now. You can report on what happened here later. Mr. Preston, how big an area do we need to seal off to catch them?"

Greg looked at his watch, then shook his head. "It's been twenty minutes. They could be miles away."

Creighton spoke up. "Assistant Chief Henderson, there are reporters outside—people must have heard shots. What are we going to say? And what can I tell the mayor about it?"

Henderson glared at him. "Tell the press we busted a drug deal that turned out to be a lot bigger than we thought. No details yet. We're still getting things straight ourselves. Captain Ryzinsky, make damn sure no one gets in here. Anyone does, you arrest them on anything you can think of. And make sure the medical people keep their mouths shut."

"Yes, sir." Ryzinsky hurried off. Creighton hesitated a moment, and Henderson glared at him. The mayor's aide turned to follow Ryzinsky.

"I can't stand that wimp Creighton," Henderson said. "Preston, you're sure we can't seal them in the area?"

"No. It's just too late. Unless they've panicked and made a dumb mistake, I don't think Sergeant Meyer and his men will find them, either."

"So, what do you suggest?"

Greg shook his head. "Not sure. They won't fall into another trap. My best guess is they'll hole up and hide for a while."

The paramedic finally managed to bandage Diaz's face, and the SWAT lieutenant held one hand over the dressing. "Preston, we have got to find these things. Where do we look?"

"I think I said only yesterday you can't hunt them down—you can't look into every sewer, basement, and hole in the L.A. basin," Greg said. "But I suppose that's what you have to try."

23

Given the total unbelievability of the situation, Greg was surprised at how quickly and smoothly Henderson got things organized.

"Ride with me, Mr. Preston," Henderson said. "I've activated the EOC, which has the old CDC, Central Dispatch Center, in it, in the sub-basement of City Hall East. We'll go back there. I imagine your lady friend will be glad to see you in one piece."

Greg nodded. "What's EOC stand for?"

"It's our old Emergency Ops Center. It's a secure bunker under City Hall East. Actually, they renamed it DOC, the Department Operations Center, but no one calls it that. They were going to close it when the new Metro CDC opened, but we convinced the city to keep it for emergency backup. We used it some during the riots after George Floyd."

"I follow you so far."

"Most people have forgotten it's there or assume it's just storage. That's one of the nice things about it. The other is that it's a bunker four stories down. Anyway, it's been activated so we can keep this operation secure from anyone who doesn't need to know—other cops included. Everybody here needs to get some rest right now, but first thing in the morning, we'll have the search going."

They drove to City Hall East, a relatively modern office building. It contrasted sharply with its close neighbor, the neo-classical monolith of City Hall, although not as much as the PAB did. They headed down to the fourth sublevel, where Julie embraced Greg as soon as he stepped off the elevator.

"How many of them did we get?" she asked.

"Seven."

"How many left?"

"Two—if we're lucky."

An energetic Hispanic woman whose uniform identified her as Captain Montoya came up and greeted the Assistant Chief. "Sir, do we still have an Unusual Occurrence in progress?"

Henderson managed a thin smile. "A UO? More like a UFO. You're damn right we still have one." He glanced at his smartphone and clicked on something. "Captain, show our visitors to the bunkroom. I'll meet the A Watch duty captain, RHD commander, SWAT commander, and Metro commander at zero six hundred in the briefing room."

"Yes, sir," the captain said. She gestured to Greg and Julie to come along. "You guys are lucky. There didn't use to be a bunkroom here. After nine-eleven, we found out in the panic that we needed one, and it only took twenty years to get it." She shrugged. "City government in action." She gave the Assistant Chief a little grin, and he nodded with an indulgent smile.

The night passed badly. Despite his exhaustion, Greg couldn't shake the dreams about the warehouse. They came again and again, with ever-more-violent endings. He was glad when an officer came in to ask them to get ready for the morning meeting.

Greg cleaned up and shaved quickly, found one clean shirt in the duffel bag he'd been living out of all over the city, and met Julie in time to hit a table in the hallway loaded with juice, coffee, and pastries. Then, they headed for the briefing room.

The EOC's briefing room wasn't as large as the room at the PAB, and it clearly wasn't even from the same century. It had walls covered in the same gray and pink fabrics as the rest of the Center, presumably installed in an attempt to brighten up the rather dark and somber-looking warren. It didn't help much.

Most of the cops were already assembled. This time, Henderson hadn't been able to keep the other brass out, and there were dark blue dress uniforms and gold braids all over the place. No one bothered to introduce Greg and Julie.

Captain Ryzinsky sketched out the plan.

"The task force under Assistant Chief Henderson will be largely organized in two-man teams," he explained. "These will be grouped into four units.

"The first unit's already working clearing the downtown construction sites. Assistant Chief Henderson thought those sites couldn't wait, being in the middle of downtown and right by the warehouse, but since they have so much underground space, he put them in four-man teams plus city workers and K-9s.

"The second unit's teams, with city utility workers, will go through the sewers and storm drains. The third unit will sweep through Griffith Park to make sure they didn't go north. Finally, the fourth unit's teams will check basements and similar hideouts in the developed areas for signs of forced entry. Units Three and Four will also have teams from the K-9 platoon. We'll keep two SWAT elements and one air unit on alert to roll to any sightings.

"You may say it's a needle-in-a-haystack problem, with less than a hundred teams searching in a city this size. That's true, but eventually, they'll either cross paths with us or be spotted and called in by citizens. The citizens won't know what they're seeing, of course, but anyone who sees a monster in his yard is pretty sure to call us. I hate to say it, but they still need to eat, so we may also find their kills and trace them that way."

"We used a fake bomb threat for the construction sites," Henderson said, "but we need another cover story. We can't hide an operation this size from the media. What would make it legitimate for SWAT teams to be poking around in building basements and sewers?"

"We do have to think of something," Creighton agreed. "If people find out what's happening, all hell would break loose. Plus, if they know these things killed four police officers, and we failed to get all of them, it could bring enormous criticism, not just on the Department, but on the Mayor and the entire…"

Greg tuned the man out, wondering what use the mayor had for such a whiner. He thought about cover stories.

"Alligators," he said aloud.

"Did you say something?" Creighton asked, looking peeved at the interruption.

"The cover story," Greg said, ignoring the mayoral flack and looking at Henderson. "For the sewers and parks, anyway. The men are looking for alligators."

Henderson looked puzzled. "What, you mean those old wives' tales about sewers having alligators in them? Who the hell would buy that?"

"You need to issue a release on it," Greg said, unperturbed. "You see, Chief, it's not a myth. An eight-foot gator was hauled out of a New York sewer and killed in 1935. It was half-frozen, but it was alive in there. Five small ones were found in 1938. Similar reports were made in 1954, 1966, and—"

"Greg, I think he gets the point," Julie said with a knowing smile. "You haven't changed a bit since college, have you?"

"Not if I could help it."

"All right, so what if there were alligators in a New York sewer?" Henderson asked.

"Easy. You announce that a city worker was attacked by an alligator in one of the sewers—just chased, maybe, no serious injury. Other workers saw a couple more of them," Greg explained, making it up as he went. "Say you don't know where they came from—get somebody from the zoo to make a statement." He paused momentarily as his mention of the zoo brought back the memory of Dr. Kerns's death.

"Anyway, the zoo can say something about how they might have been illegal pets released, or whatever. They like warmth, so the climate here's perfect—better than New York, that's for sure. All citizens are warned to stay out of the sewers and so forth. It's more of a stretch for basements, but we can try it. Have people call the police if they think anything's moving in building basements. Maybe tomorrow, just to prove the story, you sneak a small gator into one of the sewers and let the press film you dragging it out."

Creighton gave a little shrug. "Well, it might work, at least until somebody talks. And someone will, I'm afraid. We have too many people in the know already. The medical people especially scare me to death on that. We have to be ready for damage control when this leaks."

"That's your area, Mr. Creighton," Henderson said. "For now, it's the best story we have. Mr. Preston, will you work on a draft? Put in that New York stuff you were just talking about. Then Mr. Creighton and his staff can polish it up and issue it."

"Sure."

"We'll try it," Creighton said. "I'll have to inform the mayor."

"You do that," Henderson said. "We'd better call Animal Control, too. We'll need another story in case someone calls them instead of us. I'll take care of that one."

When they left the room, Greg and Julie found themselves tagging behind the rest of the group. She put a hand softly on his shoulder. "You don't always have to be the smartest person in the room, you know."

Greg raised an eyebrow. "Is that what I was doing?"

"Greg, we all have our own...I don't know if 'insecurities' is too strong a word, but we all have ways we make ourselves feel secure and in control. Ever since I've known you, yours has been to make sure you know more than anyone else and that everyone else knows it."

"You make me sound pretty annoying."

"It's not annoying to me. Okay, once in a while. But I think it's true."

"How come all those years and you never mentioned my major irritating quirk?"

"Maybe part of it was being in love, but most of it was that my irritating quirks, as you put it, were a lot worse."

"I never noticed any."

"Men are blind to a woman's quirks if they like her. Or maybe even if they just think she's pretty. God, I look back and I was a bitch."

"So why bring this up now when we're in an unbelievable situation, and we might soon be dead?"

"I have absolutely no idea."

Greg shrugged. Her comment had stung him a little but also made him think about how right she was. "That's as good an answer as any."

"I'm not complaining. It was nice in college having a guy who knew everything to study with. Besides, you were the only man I ever met who could quote Emily Dickinson without making it sound like you'd memorized her just to impress me."

"As much as I've always liked poetry, I did exactly that sometimes."

"I suspected that. But I like Dickinson, so I let you keep doing it."

"I see. Let's find an office and write some B.S."

* * *

A half-hour later, Julie looked up from the draft on Greg's laptop and nodded. "It sounds convincing to me. But how long can you get away with it? The press in this town is crazy. They'll follow the police teams, badger them half to death, and eventually get someone to talk."

"It probably won't last very long. We just have to give it our best shot."

They were jammed in a tiny cube of an office off the briefing room. It seemed like a space that had been left almost by accident by the construction, or maybe intended as a closet, but it did pick up the wi-fi installed in the complex. There were still cops in the briefing room, and Greg had shut the door for silence. They sat at a little metal table strewn with pens, legal pads, and Diet Pepsi bottles surrounding the computer.

"Time to get this to Creighton," he said. He glanced at the card Creighton had given him with his email address, then opened an email program and sent the text. Out of habit, he punched in the address for EarthLink and waited for his inbox to show up.

"What the hell?"

Julie leaned over his shoulder. "What?"

"Email from Kerns," Greg said. "Remember I gave him my address? It's time-stamped the evening he died, but I wonder how he sent it? He must have followed us right from the coroner's."

"He must have sent it from his smartphone," Julie said. "What did he say?"

Greg scanned the message. "Short notes—he must have just been typing to me while waiting in the car. These look like just unedited thoughts."

He started reading out loud. "Key question—where are they? Search for footprints at estate. If enough samples, can differentiate and ID individuals. Plot all known and possible sightings. Seem to be pack animals and, I think, highly territorial. Nothing to indicate migration. Will find den, defend territory best they can. Best chance for hunting is to flush out, keep moving. Will send more later."

"What do you think?" Julie asked. "Even if they're not moving right now, that still means the police have to cover an awful lot of places."

"I know," Greg admitted. "But what Diaz said in the briefing sounds better the more I think about it, especially after reading this from Kerns. The chances of a cop team actually finding them are slim. But if Kerns was right, and all these things just want to do is find someplace dark and hide, we don't want to let them do that."

"You always try to get the opposing counsel out of their comfort zone," Julie said. "You want to introduce a question or a piece of evidence they don't expect and make them react to you. So, in this case, we want to keep them moving."

"Exactly. Spreading out from the center, the cops have to come somewhere near them. They detect the pursuit and run. Sooner or later, they have to be seen—I hope. And the more they get chased, the more likely they are to get tired or mad enough to get careless."

Julie smiled. "I'm not as dumb as I look, you know."

"You never looked dumb to me."

"I used to feel dumb next to you. I envied you! You seemed to get everything so easily."

"If I was so smart, I wouldn't have left, would I?"

"I don't know. That all seems like another lifetime ago." Her smile vanished. "You know, I don't think I've prayed—really prayed —since I was a little girl, and nuns were standing over me to make sure I did it right. Not until this started. I prayed at Walt's funeral. And I prayed my heart out last night that you'd come out of that warehouse alive."

"Maybe someone listened. I did walk out."

"And I prayed in thanks for that. And then I got madder than hell and asked why faith didn't protect Gary Fernandez from having his throat ripped out. I didn't get an answer, either."

"Well, I don't have one. I don't think very deep sometimes. "

"Sometimes we're all afraid to think too deep." Her voice was trembling.

Greg leaned against her, which was hard not to do in the cramped space, and put an arm around her shoulders.

"Greg, I don't understand anything right now. You want to know what answer I really want?" She looked at him from scant inches away, her face so intense Greg felt uncomfortable maintaining eye contact. He broke the gaze by shaking his head.

Her face tensed up even more, and she held his shirt in both hands. "I want to know this," she said. "I loved Walt. I still love Walt, and I miss him. And, dammit, like I said before, I love you, you adolescent, self-centered—whatever. How the hell is that possible? How can I do that to him?"

They didn't embrace so much as they just slumped against each other, clutching, holding tight.

"I don't know," was all he could say. He felt pain-hot tears running down his neck from her face. "People are complicated. Including us."

Time faded away, and the tears eventually did as well. Their gazes met again.

"Maybe Walt *was* you," she whispered. "A more mature you, a steadier you. Maybe that's why you were friends. God, listen to me. I sound like my old psych prof—and he was an idiot."

She tilted her head up. "I haven't even asked if you're seeing someone these days."

"Right now, no. I've had no trouble meeting women—it's funny how some people are impressed with writers, even ones they've never heard of. But no one who's made me think, 'Wow, I want to spend my life with this person.'"

"Greg, do you love me?"

He answered before he thought about it. "Yes."

She nodded. "I guess I loved you even before you came back, but I couldn't believe I did. I'm still trying to figure out how I can love two men at once—I mean, really love them both?"

Greg started to take a stab at an answer, but she kept talking, her voice speeding up. "I know—you don't know. I don't expect you to be able to figure it out more than I can figure out why a supposedly mature professional attorney is losing it so completely."

"You're not losing it," he said. "Do you have any idea what kind of guts you showed last night when you took on that monster with nothing but a piece of wood to save a cop in a dark alley?"

"I don't know what that was or how I did it. God, that was awful—not just what happened, but that it had to be Alan. He died for us, Greg. They both did."

Greg nodded. "That's one more reason why we have to get these things. We have to stop this killing—or, at least, we have to help however we can."

"I think we've had this part of the conversation before."

Greg nodded. "And it came out the same way. We have to go on, somehow. What's between us is something we're not going to sort out until this mess is over. Neither one of us can think straight."

"Have we ever?"

"Beats me."

"Then let's not try too hard. Like you said, we've got work to do."

Greg checked the clock on the computer screen. "Yes, we do. We need to make the eleven o'clock meeting to brief Diaz's hunter-killer teams. After that, let's call up a city map and do some more thinking."

* * *

The briefing was a surreal experience. The EOC had an auditorium, small but adequate, with rows of folding chairs now occupied by stunned cops. Close-up photos of the dead korrigans were passed endlessly from hand to hand, providing the perfect attention-getter.

Greg heard the comment of one cop, a Black veteran with a lot of gray in his hair, as he looked at a photo. "I feel like those pilots who were told they were going to shoot a giant ape off the Empire State Building," he told his partner. "Who's going to do patrol when they declare the whole department fifty-one-fifty and ship us to China-town for the shrinks to study?"

Greg noticed Lt. Diaz had argued if not forced his way back to duty, though probably not without a major fight with the docs.

After Henderson brought the room to attention, Greg and Julie discussed everything they'd seen so far—how the creatures moved, how they tracked victims, how they attacked. Sergeant Meyer added his first-hand account of the carnage in the warehouse. There were lots of disbelieving looks, but no one now was willing to say the things didn't exist or a mistake had been made.

"Listen up!" Hendrickson said. "Some special precautions here."

The laptop projector came on again, showing a feed of a brunette woman of about forty in a lab coat.

"I'm Dr. Kantner," she said. "I'm the infectious disease chief at County-USC. It's been a crazy time over here. Mr. Preston asked me to ship a dead monster over there to show you, but that was a lousy idea. Every species has its own zoo inside it. Something as weird as this is guaranteed to have new bugs in it. It might have new diseases and even new parasites. The injured officers in quarantine here look healthy so far but are on broad-spectrum antibiotics plus antivirals as a prudent precaution."

Greg glanced over at Lieutenant Diaz, wondering what they'd pumped into him when he argued his way out.

Dr. Kanter continued. "So out in the field, if you have to touch one of these things, you do it with gloves. Wear N95s whenever you're in close proximity. Questions?"

"I sure as hell don't intend to let 'em get that close," a cop near Greg whispered.

There were no questions, and Henderson thanked the doc and ended the call.

"One last item before you get your marching orders," Henderson said. "Anyone who says a single word outside this task force—to a reporter, to your spouse, to a fellow officer—or to a civilian—has no career left. None. If this turns up on X or whatever, I will stomp your face until you need a new profile. Is that understood?" Heads nodded. "Then get ready, and for God's sake, be careful."

As the cops listened to Henderson, Greg was studying a hard-copy city map he'd asked a cop for on the way in. Julie watched his finger as he tapped locations. The estate. Walt's apartment. Martin's office. The coroner's office. McGraw's house. Fernandez's apartment. Lear's place. Except for Lear's house, everything since the estate had been in the city of Los Angeles itself.

"No movement," Greg whispered. "I'm more sure all the time Kerns was right. They'd been down in the city before—"

"Something to add, Mr. Preston?" Henderson asked.

Greg raised a hand in apology. "Sorry for interrupting, sir. I thought I was being quiet. But I have a better idea where to look."

"Out with it."

"They are territorial animals. They don't want to migrate. They stayed near the dolmen as long as possible. Then they moved to find a den, a hideout, in the one place they'd been before—the city itself, when they came after Walt and Martin, and so on. They're so rattled I'm sure they'd get out of the city if they had a chance, but they want to find Julie and me, too. I'd bet they're probably within a few miles of us."

Henderson nodded. "Not much of a help, but some. Okay, we'll pull in the search area we planned a bit."

Henderson nodded to Greg and Julie to join him as he headed out. When they had passed out into the hallway, he stopped. "If you guys don't mind, we'd like you to just camp out here. There won't be any privacy, but we have bunks and showers and stuff, and we don't have to worry about your safety. If you need stuff from your apartment or something, go down the hall to CDC and ask for a Sergeant Corliss. He's the liaison for anything you need."

After the cops had deployed, Julie decided to take Henderson up on his offer. Greg let her go, figuring she was safe with a cop in daylight, and instead opted for further research. He returned to his laptop and started running internet searches for university professors and authors with expertise in ancient English folklore.

About the time he had a list made up, Julie was back. She carried two suitcases and some large bags from a local Wal-Mart. Greg thought she looked more harried than when she'd left, if that was possible.

He had no idea where to put the suitcases, so he helped her shove them under the worktable in their mini-office. Julie dropped the bags on the table and shook her head.

"We picked up some stuff we thought you might need," she said. "I know you didn't bring much out."

"Julie, what's wrong?"

"My car, Greg. Three years of payments left on that car, and they tore the inside to pieces. I guess they were following our scent." She gave him a hopeless look. "What the hell do I tell the insurance company?"

"'Hello, Farmers? Bet you've never seen this.'"

"Not funny."

"Sorry. But the car can be replaced. You can't. Let's not worry about cars."

"You're right. That wasn't the only thing, though. There were about five voicemails from my mom. Thank God she always forgets my cell phone. I'll call back when I know she's out for her volunteer work and see how well I can lie that everything's all right."

"That's the only thing you can do for now."

"I know. So, what have you been doing?"

"Making a list of everyone I can find who might know something about korrigan legends. I don't want to email them first. They'd just think it was a kook. Talking to them at least gives us a chance to get a word in. Want to help me make phone calls?"

"Let's get to it."

* * *

By evening, Greg and Julie had two legal pads of notes, plus over a hundred pages of emailed and faxed (much of the material was dated long before the digital era) articles and book chapters related to korrigans. It had been easier to start conversations than he thought. Most of the experts were surprised by the interest in a fairly obscure subject, but they had bought the explanation that Greg and Julie were scriptwriters working on a movie idea. That fit in with the L.A. phone number they gave out for faxes, although, of course, none of their correspondents would know the fax machine was in the EOC.

When the B Watch officers came in at half past five, the two consultants repeated their briefing on the korrigans. The reaction was the same. Everyone started at the photos, but a lot of the officers could still only half-believe what they were assigned to do.

At five and then again at six, everyone not otherwise occupied, Greg and Julie included, gathered around a TV for the local news. Delvecchio was on again, ready to enlighten the city with words that sounded fresh from Mount Sinai.

However, he didn't have much to enlighten people with, and his lead sentence at six was the same as it had been an hour earlier. "Still no names, no clarifications from the Los Angeles Police Department concerning the deadliest shootout in the Department's history," the anchor intoned. "All we have of this story is that the police had notice of a confrontation between two drug-dealing gangs. When the police surrounded the scene and attempted to arrest the suspects, the results were tragic. As we reported earlier, four police officers are known to be dead. The Department will not comment on how many suspects were killed or arrested at the scene. The police insist that release of further information would, quote, hamper an ongoing investigation, unquote."

A video clip came up on the screen, pointlessly showing a police spokesman saying "no comment" to every question he was asked.

"As you can see, the police continue to be uncooperative," the anchor continued. "But our Karen Montrose reports that even the little information released is open to question."

The scene cut to Montrose, standing in the broad green sward in front of the PAB, a slight breeze tugging at the edges of her perfectly coifed blonde hair.

"John, there are indeed questions," Montrose said. "The warehouse where the shootout took place was actually under police control ever since its owners were arrested in June and charged with using the site for fencing and drug dealing. It's been speculated the police were actually attempting to run a sting operation. If they were, and it went disastrously wrong, that might account for the Department's unwillingness to discuss the situation."

"Well, she doesn't know anything, but I love her hair," Julie said. Her voice was acidic.

The anchor reappeared. "Karen, you have many contacts within the police department," he said. "What are they telling you?"

"Well, John, police tend to close ranks any time one of their own has been killed. No one I know would give me many details, although I have picked up hints that there was, indeed, more to this story than a drug bust that turned violent. I talked to two people who treated the injured, and all they'd say was they'd been threatened with arrest if they said anything at all."

"All right," the anchor said. "I know you'll keep on top of this." He turned back to the audience, smiling in a grave sort of way. "That's all we know at this hour. We'll keep you updated on this tragic story as information comes in."

"You said you'd met that reporter," Julie said. "What do you think? Is she just guessing?"

"I think so. The idea of a sting gone wrong could be a logical supposition on her part, or it could be something Creighton leaked to send reporters off on another false trail. Maybe it'll keep her barking up the wrong tree for a while. I notice there was no story on the police search going on today."

"The killing of four officers is so big that everyone on the police beat is trying to sniff out leads," Julie suggested.

"Reporters," a cop next to them snorted. "Parasites, all of 'em. They ought to take them all out and shoot them. Them and the lawyers, of course."

Greg saw a little gleam in Julie's eye.

"Hey, do you know why they're using lawyers to replace lab rats?" she asked.

"No," the cop said. "Why?"

"Three reasons. There are more lawyers in America than there are rats, lab workers never get emotional about hurting lawyers, and there are some things rats won't do."

The cop laughed. "That's good. Who told you that one?"

"Our graduation speaker in law school."

The officer beat a hasty retreat. "Uh, sorry, ma'am, nothing personal."

"I'll remember that if you ever need an attorney," she managed to smile.

Sergeant Corliss, an older, beefy white man with a sunburned face, stuck his head into the auditorium. "Preston! Sperling!"

Greg stood up. "Yes?"

"Captain wants you. We've got a sighting."

24

Ryzinsky was in CDC, talking rapid-fire to his officers by radio on a secure channel. When he noticed Greg and Julie, he nodded and held a hand up. He finished giving orders into the microphone, then turned to his two consultants.

"What are the details?" Greg asked.

"Janitor leaving a building on La Cienega. Heard noises like someone busting in a door. Then someone ran out of the basement entrance. It was dark, but she said it looked like two little Black kids. Search teams are converging now."

He scowled. "There's an angle I hadn't thought of. In the dark, a Black kid the right size could be mistaken for one of these things and get shot." He grabbed the mic again and urged all his search teams to be certain of their quarry.

He turned back to Greg and Julie. "That's all we'd need, isn't it? Shoot some innocent Black kid, and we're right back to Ferguson."

Greg stared at one of the city maps in the room as if he could see through the paper to the actual location. There were no video screens or electronic maps in the old bunker. The radio was full of teams coordinating movements but nothing about seeing suspects. Greg felt as nervous as if he were on the spot. He could picture the officers probing the basements and sewers as the evening shadows lengthened. Each moment could bring death in those shadows, either to the hunted or the hunters.

Then, a new voice came over the speaker. "This is Sixty-David." The voice sounded familiar to Greg—Sergeant Meyer, he thought. "We have apprehended two Black juveniles who were trespassing."

Greg considered laughing but thought better of it.

"Think how those kids must have felt when a dozen SWAT cops racked them up," Ryzinsky said. "You'd better get used to this, though. I can guarantee there'll be more false alarms before we hit the real thing."

Everyone looked for chairs and sat down, the adrenaline slowly draining away. Finally, as midnight approached, Greg and Julie gave it up and headed for the bunkroom.

As Henderson had warned, there wasn't any privacy once the deployment was in full swing. The ever-efficient Sergeant Corliss had put placards on two bunks to reserve them, but that wasn't much space with twenty cops filling the other bunks, not to mention a few officers sleeping on the floor.

Greg and Julie did get to sleep, though. They arose early Wednesday morning and spent the next few hours on chairs in the back of the CDC, talking quietly, reviewing theories, and watching the efficient but fruitless routine of the police operation.

"Not very thrilling, is it?" Julie asked. "Like watching a case drag on and wondering if it's ever going to get to trial."

"Or standing at the end of some weird assembly line," Greg suggested. "Everybody's doing their jobs as best they can, but you have no idea whether a car will roll off at the end."

"You need to take a break from writing," she smiled. "You're starting to really reach for your metaphors."

"If you read the critics, that's not news," Greg said. "The guy for the *Bee* who reviewed my last novel called me a 'modestly successful hack.'"

"You do all right. I've seen your sales figures."

Greg raised an eyebrow. "And just how did you do that?"

"It's not secret information. Especially when your law firm repre-
sents the two largest independent bookstores left in L.A."

"You really followed my career? Since when?"

"Since your first book, of course, you idiot. Three science books
and two novels, all hitting Top Ten on their Amazon categories.
You're not Dean Koontz, but you're not doing badly."

Greg found himself both intrigued and flattered. "You know
what's funny is, it came so easy."

"How do you mean that?"

"It's normal for a writer to work ten years or more before he can
support himself writing, and most never get there at all. I only had to
keep the day job for less than three years. Everything I've written,
fiction and nonfiction, has done pretty well."

"Maybe you have talent."

"I guess I must have some, or people have poor taste. I mean, I
work hard at this. But it's weird. I had planned to still be working my
way up. I was all prepared. Had a career track at Aerojet, had a ten-
year plan. When I jumped to success so fast—well, it's just strange. I
got what I wanted, and now—well, it's like something's missing."

"Greg, however you did it, don't feel bad about success. You
earned it. Along with the hundred and thirty-four grand you netted
in advances, royalties, and secondary rights last year."

Greg shook his head. "I can't keep anything secret. Maybe I'd
better switch lawyers."

"I don't come cheap."

"You'd be worth it, I'm sure."

Julie smiled, more with her eyes than with her lips. "That was the
old college line, right? 'I'm easy, but I'm not cheap.'"

"As I recall, you were neither."

The laugh felt good for both of them.

* * *

After lunch, Greg went back to the micro-office near the briefing
room. He and Julie read over the korrigan material they had accumu-

lated. Most of it simply repeated the same basic sources. "Hard to get new data when all the writers on the subject have been dead eight hundred years," Greg said.

Sergeant Corliss located them. "Time to take you guys for a little ride," he said. "They want the Captain and you two to see the coroner."

* * *

Dr. Sporkin met them in the familiar conference room. The scene hadn't changed much except for the presence of two extra uniformed officers who followed the coroner everywhere he went.

Greg, Julie, Diaz, Henderson, and Ryzinsky took chairs. Sporkin paced the front of the room for a moment, showing a nervousness Greg had never seen.

"It's hard to begin," he said apologetically. He took his glasses off and rubbed his eyes. "In fact, it's hard to report any of this with a straight face. I called in a friend who's a professor of biology at UCLA to help me analyze some of the findings. We still drew too many blanks to mention."

"Doctor, have you got anything useful for us?" Henderson asked. "The killings are piling up. We had another last night."

"What?" Greg and Julie asked as one.

Ryzinsky spoke. "I was going to present this all together in the next briefing because we think there are three more we can connect. But an old man just last week seemed to have disappeared on the golf course next to the park. I remember we thought it was weird because Officer Poole said they found his maintenance cart untouched, but the ground next to it was torn up, like someone had taken some of the turf. No other clues. But now we can guess what did it.

"The other was a double homicide about five miles south of the estate and incidentally about six blocks from your apartment. It was a meatpacker's place, one of the old-fashioned little mom-and-pop shops. The business was broken into, and two people were killed. Torn up. It was treated as a break-in gone bad at first, so we didn't catch it while we were still in the EOC. Wasn't till you were on the way over here that they found two bodies stuffed into a duct. But we have teams spreading out from that location now."

"Let me guess," Greg said. "Some of the meat was torn up, too."

Ryzinsky nodded.

"Wait," Julie said. "Sometimes they're going to a lot of trouble to hide bodies—they even tore up the golf course to hide the blood, it sounds like—and sometimes they don't even try. Why would that be?"

"Perps in a hurry leave a mess," Ryzinsky said. "They probably hide bodies when they have the time."

"Dr. Sporkin," Henderson said, "maybe you ought to continue."

"Thank you. I began with the theory that these creatures might be synapsids—creatures that originally were neither mammals nor reptiles, and they produced at least one primate-like species before dying out except for a branch that became the mammals. The cell structure I discussed at our last meeting made me doubt that hypothesis, but it might work. That species might have evolved further in Africa, adopting underground refuges and night hunting under pressure from competitors like the dinosaurs. Ordinary animal traders couldn't have captured them, but I understand the Romans who captured animals from the arena were superbly skilled. That at least places them in Europe."

"Could they have evolved somewhere else?" Greg asked.

"The African synapsid origin is just a guess. Given how strange some of their organs and cells are, their line may be far older, even though we've found no fossils. We know we've only found a small faction of the species that ever existed, but it still makes me uneasy. It would be like so many monster movies where they have the living dinosaur, but no one explains where it was all this time."

"Yet they came from somewhere, like places the land submerged," Greg said. "Where they might have lived, and just a remnant survived. I know the whole western coast of North America was once a lot higher than now, and Doggerland up north of England used to connect to the continent. We don't know what lived there when."

"I can imagine something like that," Sporkin said. "We have to start with just the fact they're here. But they're part of a ghost lineage, something we've never documented.

"Everything about them is strange. Hearing, smell, skeletons. The skeleton is close enough to call it vertebrate bone but not to be matched to an order or even class. There are reinforced cartilage capsules over the joints like rugby pads and a kind of network knitting together and strengthening the rib cage. The mix of cartilage and bone is so strange it made me remember an old lecture on zebrafish, where cartilage structures change shape and ossify. I've no idea what evolutionary pressures or competition were involved in their development. But however they evolved, here they are."

"So we're like those Europeans who first got hold of a platypus," Greg said. "They had no clue how such a thing existed. It just did."

"Good example. They'll write a library's worth of papers just on the lifecycle of this thing, whatever that turns out to be. We have the tools to work its evolution backwards now, but it will take time."

"When did they evolve to be murdering maniacs?" Julie asked harshly.

"We can't think that way," Greg said. "These are clever animals trying to survive. Even if we want every one of them dead, we have to remember that. If we think of them as mindless killers, we'll never figure out their actions."

"Whatever they are, this is one of the great days in the history of science," Sporkin replied. "Every scientific institute in the world will be breaking the door down to get a look at these creatures."

"You haven't told anyone," Henderson said.

"Of course not. Only four of us, counting my professor friend I'd trust with my life, have seen the bodies, and all are sworn to secrecy."

Diaz spoke up. "If you're done admiring these things, would you mind telling us how to find them and kill them?"

Sporkin hesitated. "That's something we need to discuss," he said, looking at Henderson. "I know the damage the korrigans have done, but I think these are a species and a lineage totally unknown. We need to study live ones, not just dead ones."

"What the hell do you want me to do?" Henderson asked. "I've got at least eleven people dead so far in a city it's my duty to protect. We try to catch them alive, and there'll be more deaths. Forget it, Doc."

"There's got to be a way," Sporkin said.

"That's what Dr. Kerns thought," Greg interjected.

"Philip was good," Sporkin said. "He was also my friend. But he didn't have any idea what he was dealing with. This has to be planned very carefully, but it's got to be done. The LAPD has to stop using lethal means for this hunt."

"Excuse me, Doctor Sporkin." Julie's face was tight with barely suppressed anger. "These things are out to kill us and probably you. If it's us or them that gets killed next, I vote for them."

"Ditto," Greg said. "Doctor, I'm a science writer when I'm not doing sasquatch novels. I want to further human knowledge, and I understand how monumental this is. But I'm not willing to die for it. Are you forgetting you're a public official? You have the same duty as the police—protect the citizens first."

"All right, I'll allow that I may be underestimating the challenge here," Sporkin said. "It is hard for a humble medical examiner to look at scientific immortality without wanting to it. But please, if at all possible, attempt to leave at least one alive."

"If the men who find them were in that warehouse," Henderson said, "that might be damn tough. I will tell them if they have one crippled and if there's no danger, not to finish it off. But that's all I'll do, and I don't think that scenario is likely to happen."

Sporkin nodded. "I'll just have to hope we get lucky. In the meantime, I assume you'd like some more information."

"All you have."

"Let's start with the senses," Greg said. "Sight and smell."

"I can't say exactly how good their senses are without tests on live subjects, but I can tell some things. First, the eyes. The structures in the eyes are similar to ours. There are rods and cones like in human eyes, but the individual cells are smaller and more densely packed. I would guess their night vision is on par with the best nocturnal mammals.

"Smell is harder to judge. Somewhere this damn thing evolved specialized cells with deep pore-like openings distributed over much of the face, in contrast to our large nostrils. Breathing passes air through those holes, although the main volume of air goes through an arc-shaped opening around that natural trochanter. By the sheer number of pores and specialized cells packed around each, I suspect the overall scent capability is at least in the wolf class."

"Is that better or worse than a bloodhound?" Ryzinsky asked.

"Better."

"Not very helpful so far," Greg said. "How about hearing?"

"Not as good as ours, I don't think," Sporkin said. "There are two external ears, but they're small and almost flat against the head. You can hardly see them in the hair. By the way, that's not actually hair. They have skin filaments like the so-called 'hairy frogs.'"

The group spent two more hours in deep discussion, going over all Sporkin had learned from bodies, and all Greg had learned from legends.

Korrigans, Sporkin reported, apparently reproduced sexually. All the bodies obtained so far showed the same organs, apparently male. The breeding habits of the species remained unknown. "Some animals breed according to season. Others can wait until they think it's safe and the female has found a secure location," Sporkin said. "So we have no idea whether they will breed soon—or have already bred."

"What's the most likely hiding spot?" Henderson asked, his tone weary.

"They might like sewers, and they might not," Sporkin said. "So many chemicals and smells down there they haven't been exposed to —and with those noses."

"Maybe that's another case of looking at what they didn't do," Julie said. "You'd think they'd have gone into the park. All they'd have to do is cross the banks and the golf course. Or go east until they crossed Commonwealth and then north."

"Roosevelt Municipal Golf Course," Ryzinsky said.

"Maybe there's something there they didn't like—think of all the things they treat golf courses with. Where was that man killed?"

"By the fence on the south side. The fence right next to the museum."

"You may be right," Greg said to Julie. "They reconned the golf course, but something—the herbicides, insecticides, whatever—didn't sit well with them. If I remember Walt's plans, the drainage goes along Commonwealth, too. So they decided to try south."

"I'll bet they're in the storm drains," Ryzinsky said. "They connect into the regular sewers, but it's not like you can just wander around down there. There are all kinds of grates and locks and stuff."

"That's a thought," Henderson said. "Tell all the search teams underground to report any barriers that have been broken open. As you might expect, Chief Aldridge wants daily briefings, so set those up through me."

There was a knock, and the door opened. A female officer entered and nodded to Henderson. "Sir, one of the task force patrols just called in. They said they found a one-eighty-seven. He was all ripped up."

25

They moved in a heavily armed three-car convoy. There was still a little evening light as the group headed south on the Harbor Freeway. Greg, Julie, and Sporkin were packed in the back seat of the center car. The officer riding shotgun leaned close to hear the radio, then twisted around to talk to the passengers.

"That was the RHD detectives on scene. They said the body looks fresh."

"Any other details?" Greg asked.

The cop shook his head. "I don't like to break in while the brass are all talking at once like they are now. You'll know pretty quick. It's just a couple of blocks ahead."

A minute later, they were on a typical street of shabby, barred-window shops and apartments. There was a disco display of flashing lights just ahead.

The driver braked hard, and everyone piled out. Despite the crowd of police, Greg felt for the forty-five he carried in a shoulder holster. He'd never worn such a holster before and could never get the rig adjusted right, but it made him feel a little better. Julie, he noted, had the clasp of her purse open, which was probably the best way to get at her pepper spray if she needed to.

They stepped over a line of yellow police tape and caught up with Henderson. The police crowd parted in front of the Assistant Chief, and they looked down at the body.

It was the corpse of a medium-sized Black male, dressed in what might have been a uniform of light blue short-sleeved shirt and black jeans. There was some kind of badge on the man's chest, and a collapsible baton was a few feet away, already outlined in chalk. The badge was unreadable because of the blood and eviscerated organs covering the man's torso.

Greg fought down his nausea and listened as Henderson quizzed the cops on the scene. The victim was a private security guard from a company hired by a group of shop owners to patrol this area. The killing had been called in just a half-hour ago, but no one could be found who'd seen it happen.

One detective showed how he'd traced the movements involved. The guard had come out from a narrow alley between two shops—running, to judge by his footprints in the dust. There were some other marks, too—smaller, stubbier footprints showing only four toes.

"You can see that basement window's broken," the detective was saying. "I figure the guard saw the suspect breaking in. Suspect runs this way, guard chases him. Either the asshole turns and gets the guard right here where the alley opens, or another suspect is waiting here that gets him. Guard walks a few feet—you can see the blood starts here—but that's as far as he gets."

"He stumbled out onto the sidewalk," Greg conjectured. "There was nobody right there, but cars were passing, and it's not really dark yet. The korrigans took off."

"Where?" Henderson asked.

"That's the question. There could be a hideout close by—I'd kind of suspect that, from them being in this area so early in the evening."

Henderson nodded to Ryzinsky. "Set up a perimeter and sweep the area," he said. Then he gestured at Dr. Sporkin. "Care to pronounce, Doc?"

Despite his career of exposure to human carnage, the doctor

seemed a little shaky as he glanced at the body. "Consider him pronounced."

* * *

They stayed in the area for another two hours while the police teams searched, guns at the ready. When nothing became apparent, Henderson ordered the group back to the EOC.

They got there in time for the eleven o'clock news. Creighton was there to watch with them.

"We had to put out the alligator story this afternoon," he said. "We were getting too many calls from reporters about police seen in sewers and basements. It played okay so far on the internet, but let's see how the local news likes it."

The anchor on tonight was not Delvecchio, but a younger man with blow-dried hair and startlingly white teeth. After the repetitive scenes of reporters complaining the LAPD was still stonewalling on the warehouse story, the anchor showed his dazzling smile to the audience said, "The police do have another concern tonight—one that's less serious but no less strange. Here's Karen Montrose."

Montrose did a quick standup, then cut to a tape of Creighton speaking to a crowd of reporters in the lobby at the PAB. Greg had to admire Creighton's performance. He was smooth and seemed utterly convincing. He had a zoo veterinarian beside him who commented how the sewers in L.A. would be a survivable environment for alligators and issued a warning about the dangers of approaching the unpredictable reptiles.

"That's the word here at police headquarters, Kevin," Montrose smiled. "It sounds as unusual to me as it undoubtedly does to our viewers, but one might say that this is Los Angeles after all. Certainly, the police officers going into the sewers with shotguns are deadly serious.

"They say it's too dangerous for reporters to go down there with the police. We hope to persuade them to change their minds on that. Certainly, our viewers deserve a look at a story as bizarre as this one."

"Thank you, Karen." The anchor turned back to the camera. "And that's the information so far on the great Los Angeles alligator scare," he concluded, his smile broader than before. "We'll keep you up to date as this scaly story slithers along."

"Well, they seem to believe it so far," Julie said.

"They seem to," Greg said, nodding. "Something about Montrose bugs me, though. She's not quite buying it."

"I think you're overestimating her," Julie said.

"Maybe. But she's been doing the serious stories on the killings. This is a feature. If she did it, it's because she wanted to. She smells something."

He paused. "I wonder what would happen if the story did break. Do even murderous cryptids get people's attention here, or would everyone just say, 'Like, wow, man,' and head for the beach?"

"You mean, would people just offer them a joint?" Julie asked. "I wish I could laugh at that. Right now, I want a joint for the first time since I quit them in law school."

Just as they headed for the bunkroom, an officer tapped Greg on the shoulder. "Phone for you," he said. "Said it's urgent."

Greg scowled. "Huh. Must be another police official."

The cop shrugged and pointed to a phone on a nearby desk. "Line four."

Greg picked it up. "Yes?"

"Mr. Preston, this is Karen Montrose."

"What the hell do you want? And how did you find me?"

"Never mind how I found you. Just say I have a lot of contacts. Look, I want to know what's really happening here. You come in because you were friends with Walt Rivas, who was murdered. Then in the next few days, you're at Rob Martin's murder scene, there's the warehouse fight no one will talk about, and cops are poking all over the city with this bullshit alligator story. This smells, and it smells like it's all connected. Look, the people have a right to know what's going on."

"People, my ass," Greg said. "You don't care about the people. You'd sell your grandmother for a five-point rise in the overnights."

"That's unfair, Greg, and it's not true. But I didn't call to debate journalistic ethics. I'm a reporter, and you have a story you have no right to conceal."

"I'll tell you a story," Greg snapped. "There's a story about someone in the LAPD who gave out information he shouldn't and should be prosecuted for it. Why don't you do that story instead of playing God, or goddess, about what the public should know and what they shouldn't?"

"Greg, think about how important this is," she pressed. "Police officers have been killed."

Greg opted to try a reasonable approach. "It's not for me to discuss," he said.

"Unless you are ready for me to tell everyone about the murderous unknown animals you're trying to track down, we need to discuss it."

Greg closed his eyes. She knew something.

"What can I do to persuade you to do what's right instead of what gets ratings?"

"Sometimes they're the same thing. Look, we only met once, but I trust you. And you need to trust me. Do you know the Pantry on Figueroa?"

"Sure, I remember it."

"Meet me for breakfast at eight tomorrow. Just you. I think I have a solution for both of us."

"I'll be there." Greg's voice was calm, but his knuckles were gripping the receiver so hard they hurt.

"I'll see you then. Good night."

Greg slammed down the phone.

He was suddenly aware Julie's face was pressed against his so she could hear. "How could she possibly have put all this together?" she asked.

"I don't know," Greg said. "But I need to meet her. And before we get any rest tonight, somebody has to find Creighton and tell him his cover story's been shot to hell."

* * *

They talked with Creighton, who reluctantly agreed Greg had to meet the reporter. "I wouldn't tell anyone else for now," he said. "Keep it between us." He grinned. "By the way, we managed to buy a five-foot gator from a reptile farm and smuggle it into town. We're going to drag it out of a sewer in the morning. Hopefully, that'll help some."

Eventually, they got to bed. "Starting to agree with that one cop about journalists," Greg mumbled as he sank, exhausted, onto his cot.

"And lawyers?" Julie asked.

"Not all of you. Maybe the ones who defend reporters."

* * *

The next morning, Creighton escorted Greg out of the building. "Good luck," the PR man said.

"Thanks." Greg started walking down Figueroa toward the retro diner called the Original Pantry.

He was there at quarter till eight; fortunately, there was an open booth. He needed to wait only a few minutes before Karen Montrose came in.

She had dressed in lavender polo shirt and khaki pants. With sunglasses on, Greg thought, she would have just about succeeded in blending into the crowd if not for the aura of energetic confidence that seemed to exert a magnetic tug on everyone she passed close by. The men took long looks at her, but most of the women also spared a glance.

She slid into the booth and gave him an unnaturally bright smile, sliding her sunglasses off and setting them aside. An attentive waiter materialized as if he'd popped out of the floor. Karen ordered a diet cola and three pancakes. As the waiter turned to hustle away, she tapped his arm and pointed at Greg. Greg placed the same order, then grinned at the blonde reporter.

"You probably think I enjoyed that," she said.

"You did."

She shrugged. "Okay, I did. How did men get all the power in the world if you never think with your brains?"

"You seem to be the one with power right now," Greg said.

The waiter reappeared in record time and set glasses in front of them. Karen's had been festooned with two lemon wedges.

When the love-struck waiter had moved on, Karen turned back to Greg. "I don't know about power," she said. "Remember what I said on the plane? I was third runner-up for Miss California, I can speak educated but unaccented English and pretty good Spanish, and I have nice boobs. That combination will get anyone on the air in this town. After that, it's all about how much you're willing to sell yourself to make a name."

"So I've heard."

"Let's get to the point," she said. "I have learned some things no one outside LAPD is supposed to know about this case. Don't ask how because I won't tell you, but you know something about research. There's always a way."

"Probably easier for you with all those hopeless men around."

"True enough," she said. "Look, there is something here for everyone. You and the cops don't want this story told right now. You may not believe this, but I understand that. At some point, though, this case is going to be over, and you will want the story told right."

"I smell an offer here," Greg said.

She nodded. "When you can talk on the record, you talk only to me. Same for Julie Sperling."

Greg tried to minimize his visible reaction to the mention of Julie's name. "I make it a rule never to try to speak for a lawyer."

"Good rule, but I suspect she'll think the way you do."

"What is it you think I'm not talking about?" Greg asked.

"I'm not going to tell you everything I know," she said. "But you won't make any deal if I don't tell you something, so here goes. We have several connected murders, and they weren't done by human beings. They were done by an animal. Whether it's something some cryptozoologist dragged back from Indonesia or something that got out of a genetic research lab, or whatever, I don't know. But no one brings an expert from the zoo to a meeting at the coroner's for ordinary murders. And when that zoo expert gets killed by whatever he's trying to stalk, we're not talking about a lost mountain lion or even an escaped tiger.

"You're in this because it killed your friend and because you're a science writer. I'm in this because it's my job."

"And because it will make your career."

"Damn right it will. But are you telling me that's wrong? To finally get ahead by doing this job better than all the people swallowing the cover stories?"

"No, it's not wrong," Greg said. "Not if you're willing to hold back a little to protect people's lives."

"Telling people about a threat is the way to save lives," she said. "Hiding it isn't.

"You know what will happen with panic. People shooting trespassers, people dying in traffic, and probably a lot more I can't think of now."

"No course of action we can take is going to save everyone," she said, with a fierce conviction that Greg thought concealed a little uncertainty.

He pressed it. "Karen, you can get rich and famous and tell the truth. But please, please, believe me, this is not the right time. The cops have a plan, and it'll work—*if* they can work quietly for a little longer."

"If someone else breaks the story on me, I'm going to kick your ass," she said.

"Thank you."

"Don't think I've shut up. I haven't heard anything that tells me anyone but me is on to this. Look, I can't promise I'll go on the air with stories that just parrot the police version of events. I'm not good at hiding disbelief. But I'll keep the specifics to myself for now—*if* I know I'm getting exclusive access when you or the police can let out the truth."

"You drive a hard bargain."

"Damn right." She flashed that smile again, and this time, there actually seemed to be a little warmth in it. "You know, we are in the same profession. I just give the short, fast version of a story, and you do it in depth. Maybe writing the whole story of this someday is something we could do together."

"I'm not thinking that far ahead. I'm thinking about getting out of this alive." Greg bit his lip as he realized he'd confirmed for her a couple of times now how serious the situation really was. "So can we trust each other?"

"My ex-husband asked that about twenty times a day for a while. He kept suspecting I had another man because I was never home. It turned out he just hoped I did since he already had another woman."

"Man had no taste."

Karen toned down the usual camera smile to a sly grin. "If you can't trust a blonde reporter on the make, who can you trust?"

"Some people would say, 'a rattlesnake,' but we need to take a chance here—both of us. I'll trust you." He was a bit surprised to hear himself saying that with meaning under the circumstances.

She nodded. "You have my card. Your cell seems to have been off lately, but you can call me, and I can email you. Let's keep in touch."

"Promise made," he said.

"Likewise."

She dropped a ten on the table and rose, turning to leave. She stopped a step later, half-turning back to him. "Greg?"

"Yes?"

"I don't know if you have other romantic entanglements, and I won't ask. But I'd at least like to be friends when this is over."

"I'd like that."

"And between now and then, remember what I said about kicking your ass. If there's one whisper that I'm going to be scooped—well, I will *not* be scooped."

"Understood."

She put her sunglasses on in one graceful movement and was gone.

Greg leaned back in the booth, looking at the space where she had just been. Was that an act of professionally-motivated flirtation, or had a truly stunning lady just indicated a personal interest in him? Either she was a good actor, or she liked writers. Under other circumstances...

She'd mentioned "other romantic entanglements" but had promised not to ask about them. *Do I have romantic entanglements?* Rightly or wrongly, he did, and it was just as well Karen hadn't asked.

* * *

Greg returned to the EOC and reported to Creighton and Julie. Both agreed he'd done well. Creighton reported there was no deluge of reporters yet. Whether Montrose knew or thought she knew, she was apparently keeping it to herself.

They watched morning show coverage of the alligator that had allegedly just been captured and was hauled out by two zoo people with nooses. Cops with heavy gloves helped them wrestle it down and duct-tape its jaws as the cameras zoomed closer.

"I know just how it feels," Julie said.

The day passed, filled with searches, false alarms, and fruitless discussions. Greg endlessly re-read his meager data and pondered maps, trying to divine some kind of inspiration.

About three in the afternoon, Ryzinsky came looking for Greg and Julie in the office where they'd been talking over korrigan legends yet again.

"It's hit the fan now," he said. "We've got another death, and this one's a celeb."

"Who?"

"That Miss America reporter, Montrose."

26

The Clan had to move.

Some were being disoriented from staying too long in the Stinking Holes. Help each other. Find a place. Find a Home Place.

Two foragers came back. There was a place. There were still Tall Ones around and strange heavy vibrations. But not far away was a place.

It was a lair for the Tall Ones but unused for a long time. It was closed above ground and extended underground. They would explore the ground around it, looking for threats and food supplies. Not the best, not a real Home Place, but a Home Place for now.

They had to have a Home Place. One of the Clan was becoming a Life Bringer. They must protect the Life Bringer. The Clan must survive.

27

Greg stood up so suddenly that he jarred the table and had to grab the laptop to stop it from sliding off. "When? How?"

"Not sure when. City utility guy found her an hour ago. Her and a cameraman, I guess. They had utility coveralls on and were down in a sewer."

"Damn it," Greg breathed. "Damn it, damn it, damn it! Where?"

"Down on South Hoover."

"That's not far from where we were last night," Julie said.

Greg turned to Julie, pain in his eyes. "And if I'd given her a better warning—told her what she was up against—she wouldn't have been there to get killed."

"Greg, don't start that on yourself," she said with a fierce look. "You know you couldn't have told her everything. The consequences would be catastrophic."

He shook his head. "I can't forget I had a chance to warn her off."

"Greg, you can't second-guess. You did what was right. No one told her to crawl into a sewer. And tell me honestly—don't you think she would have pressed on no matter what you told her?"

"Probably."

"Definitely."

"Damn it, you know what she told me?" Greg asked. "She was only thirty-one years old, or about that, and thought her career had stalled. Think about feeling desperate at thirty-one. She needed a really gigantic story to move up. Yeah, she would have gone after this no matter what."

"She was smart but too damned ambitious," Julie said. "Even I could tell that about her, and we've never met. Now all you can do now is keep trying to make sure no one else gets killed."

Greg nodded. The sliver of romantic interest he thought or imagined had passed between Karen and himself was something Julie would never hear of.

"Right as usual, Counselor. You know, you can take your own advice. Stop blaming yourself."

"For what?"

"For Walt. For getting him interested in the museum story."

"I don't blame myself."

"I think you do. I've thought that since you first mentioned it to me. But when the controversy erupted around that museum, don't you think Walt would have been curious whether you were involved or not?"

Julie nodded. "He would have been."

"Then we'll make a deal. If you promise to do the same, I'll try to let go of what I can't change—and what probably would have made no difference."

"Deal."

Greg thought about the korrigans for a minute. "One killing south of the university area, one just north," he said. "This is after the killings at the meatpackers' place near Griffith Park. So there's more of a pattern than we thought."

"They wouldn't like the school. It's too full of people," Julie said.

"Not permanently, but someplace around there might do for a while. I read there's a lot of construction going on at the school. That probably creates some new hiding places—excavations, opened conduits, and so on."

He turned to Ryzinsky, who had been silent through their

personal discussion. "Captain, we should go down and take a look. I'm going nuts here anyway, and maybe we could spot some likely hideouts."

Ryzinsky shrugged. "There's a hundred cops in that area, and it's daylight. No reason it would be dangerous. Ask Corliss to find you a ride. Tell him I said he's to stay with you at all times."

"Thanks."

* * *

Corliss found a team of officers heading for the university and joined them in heading south. They were in one of the big blue Suburbans belonging to the SWAT unit, the back loaded with gear ranging from night-vision goggles to forced-entry tools.

Corliss turned to talk to Greg as they rode. "I was at the briefing yesterday morning," he said. "Where do you really think these things are from? Outer space?"

"I don't know. It could be, I suppose. Or they came from a line of evolution that started way back before the dinosaurs. Either is a long shot, but one of them has to be true."

"Just wondering. I saw a UFO once when I was camping in Angeles National Forest. I never told anyone in the Department—I figured they'd call me crazy."

He glanced at the driver, who grinned and shrugged. "I ain't heard nothing," the other cop said.

"It was a big, red-lighted thing with no noise at all," Corliss said. "Scared me to death. You think some UFOs might be from space?"

"Same answer," Greg said. "It's possible, but we don't have evidence yet."

"I'd like to know where else it could have come from. Anyway, here we are."

The car slowed as it drove into a herd of police vehicles occupying a parking lot two blocks north of the university. They emerged from the SUV just in time to watch two ambulances pull out with the latest casualties.

Diaz noticed them. "Hell of a mess, isn't it? Never felt so damn helpless as a cop. We can't nail two lousy animals."

"Not just any animals," Greg reminded him.

They spent the next two hours walking around, accompanied by the SWAT team that drove them there. They looked all over the two major construction sites, talking to workers about possible intruders, looking in excavations, and checking fresh dirt for tracks. At five, the construction workers knocked off for the day, and Greg, Julie, and their escorts looked some more.

They were tired and dirty by the time evening came. They went back to the main police parking area to get something to drink and talk to Diaz about the next move.

As they were approaching the lieutenant, a cop signaled for his attention. "Lieutenant, Dispatch wants you."

Diaz leaned into the nearest patrol car and picked up the radio. Moments later, he straightened abruptly, tossing the radio mike away.

"Report down on the campus—someone breaking into a building. Said it looked like two Black kids! Let's move!"

"Probably was two Black kids—again," the cop next to Greg said, but no one hesitated, false alarm or no.

"It's at the International Center!" Diaz said. "Where's that?"

Greg pointed to a tall, slender tower, topped with a stylized metal globe, visible from their location. "That tower's on the right building!"

Galvanized at the prospect of finding their quarry after days of futility, the cops swarmed into action. Most left their cars where they were and headed out on foot. Others started vehicles and pulled out, intending to go around the area and close off the southern approaches to the International Center.

Greg and Julie fell in with a body of cops moving at a trot despite their heavy gear.

"Thought I'd stop by and see the place when I was in town," Greg said. "Didn't know I'd have an escort."

Corliss had been ahead of them, but now he slowed up and let them pull alongside. "If you guys are coming, stay back with me," he said. "Henderson'd have my ass if you get hurt."

"Understood."

Now the red-brick buildings of the campus rose all around them. They could see the IC, or "ICK" as the students probably still called it.

The whole school seemed alive with officers; as if a hill of ants in blue combat suits had been kicked. Greg noticed a man in the tan uniform of the campus security force staring at the avalanche of police.

"What the hell's going on?" He was demanding. "We can handle a couple of kids!"

No one answered him as the officers converged on the IC. The building had three wings forming a squared C, with a sunken court-yard in the middle. The buildings blocked out the last rays of the sun, and fingers of light from flashlights, some mounted on the SWAT officers' submachine guns, probed the narrow windows and the glass doors.

Greg, Julie, and Corliss skirted the building, trying to get the big picture of where the cops were looking and where any signs of entry might be. As they reached the south side, Greg saw a cop bend down to look into the shrubbery around the building's base. Abruptly, something flung the officer away so hard his body landed with an audible thud.

A dozen flashlights swiveled instantly. "Look!" someone yelled.

Two small figures bounded across the grass.

A quick-reacting cop swiveled his shotgun and fired from the hip. One korrigan tumbled, got up, and stumbled through a hedge, trying to keep up with the other creature.

"This way!"

Cops swarmed in from all directions. Greg had his own gun out now, and Julie had the pepper spray. Greg realized that Corliss should have pulled them back and kept them out of it, but the sergeant, too, was caught up in the chase.

"That way!" A flashlight momentarily picked out two shadows, one seemingly pulling the other along. Covered by the long, low hedges common on the campus, the creatures had ducked through the police skirmish line and were scrambling west toward the administration building.

Diaz was waving his flashlight. "Coleman, flank 'em on the north! Shuker, tell the cars to come around the west side!"

Hunters and hunted skirted the admin building on the south side. Ahead of them now loomed the massive building housing the main gym. On its far side was a street, and the first cars were pulling up there now.

There was a crash of glass.

"They've ducked into the gym!"

The pursuers split up, some surrounding the building, others smashing the glass in the twin front doors with shotgun butts to enlarge the hole the korrigans had made. The police stormed inside. Someone found the master switches, and lights came on all over the building.

The main entrance led into a long hallway, with offices and exercise rooms branching off on both sides. Greg and Julie came in behind the main body of police. There was no immediate sign of the korrigans.

"They went downstairs!" an officer in the lead yelled.

A stream of uniforms poured down the concrete steps into a maze of corridors below. As Greg remembered, a pool was down there somewhere, along with racquetball courts and countless other rooms. He and Julie had long since lost Corliss, and they tagged along with the last group of cops heading downstairs.

From below came a shout of triumph. "There!"

Greg and Julie hurried down. A few steps up from the bottom, a solid mass of cops blocked them, and they tried to peer over the officers' helmeted heads.

"They're coming!" There was an eruption of shouting and footsteps from a connecting hallway off to their left. The korrigans were being herded.

The creatures appeared, dashing into view, running full-tilt until they saw what awaited them. Then the korrigans froze, trapped in a bend of the main corridor. Behind them were two heavy, locked doors. To their left was a solid wall. In front of them and to their right were phalanxes of police.

There was a moment of unnatural quiet.

Then one korrigan sprang at the nearest cops.

The fusillade was deafening. Submachine guns, shotguns, pistols, and CAR-15 semi-automatic rifles all opened fire at once. Greg ducked back into the stairwell, pulling Julie with him and pushing her against the wall for cover as the cataclysmic noise assaulted their ears.

As suddenly as the eruption of gunfire began, it ended, and there were only echoes and moans.

Greg looked.

The tough bodies of the korrigans had been literally shredded by the hail of bullets and shot. They lay on the floor, looking like heaps of bloodstained rags in the dim light.

Greg put his gun away. He and Julie looked at each other, but neither could think of anything to say. They slumped on the cold, hard stairs and just sat there, holding each other. Greg remembered and tried to apply an old yoga trick – breathe deep, hold, slow exhale, pause – to calm the blood surging through his heart and body

Time passed, a fuzzy succession of images. Corliss talking to them, wincing as first aid was applied to an arm wounded by one of the unavoidable ricochets. Paramedics maneuvering their equipment downstairs, clanking and banging things against the walls. Sporkin talked briefly with them, the light of scientific fame glinting in his eyes even as he lamented the unfortunate deaths of the last korrigans.

Greg eventually found himself walking hand in hand with Julie out of the building. All the doors had been propped open, and they waded through the broken glass out the north entrance. They just kept going, walking away from the hubbub and the light show.

"What now?" Greg finally asked.

"I don't know. Maybe a long vacation. Somewhere where the journalists won't find us."

"We could hit Paradise Island, but maybe instead we want some-place it's too cold for korrigans. Alaska is nice this time of year." Greg squeezed her hand. "It's still hard to believe any of this happened."

"Well, everyone will know it did. Sporkin will see to that."

Neither really thought about where they were going. They passed the darkened shopping complex just north of the campus and jaywalked across 30th Street into a residential neighborhood. They could see the lights of more police cars ahead, still parked near where Karen Montrose had been found.

A dark shadow rustled through the bushes ahead of them.

Julie grabbed his arm hard. "What was that?"

Greg shook her off and started to run.

28

"Greg, no!"

The shadow flashed down 30th Street and turned into an alley. Greg clawed the pistol from its holster.

Where—there! Half a block ahead, under a lonely streetlamp, the thing bounded left, out of the gravel-paved alley. There was a thud of wood on wood. Breathless, Greg raced toward the sound.

He stopped. He was behind one of the old wooden houses that dominated the neighborhood. Most had been renovated, but this one looked neglected—abandoned, in fact.

It had a basement with ground-level windows. But the windows had been covered with plywood so long ago that the plywood and siding had been painted together. The color might once have been white, but there wasn't enough light to tell.

One panel wasn't nailed onto the house anymore. It was loose, leaning against the window frame.

The korrigans hid here, Greg thought. *And one of them—at least —hadn't been in the warehouse or in the gym.*

Greg hesitated as frustration, rage, and terror clashed in his head. Go for the cops? No, the thing would run.

His heart hammering, Greg yanked the plywood aside and looked into the well of darkness.

There was no glass left in the window. Gun in hand, Greg sat down and slid feet-first into the opening.

He grabbed at the edge to slow his descent, got his elbow wedged, yanked free, and crashed awkwardly to the floor. Gasping with the pain of a turned ankle, he struggled to his feet, straining for the noise of death.

All was silent.

Greg's eyes adjusted to the gloom as best they could. He was in a basement workshop and/or storeroom filled with cobwebbed shelves. He half-looked, half-felt along the nearby shelving. His hand closed on a box that felt familiar. It was filled with wooden matches. Greg eagerly picked it up.

He had the box open when a blur of fury hit him on the right shoulder with a force like a speeding car. Greg spun completely around, crying out in pain as he bounced off a wall of shelves and clutched instinctively for support. He staggered against a water heater, some part of his brain signaling frantically that he had lost his gun. He grabbed a short piece of two-by-four, knowing it was useless, feeling pain continue to shoot through his arm from the shoulder.

There were sounds. Stealthy sounds, and movements half-seen and half-imagined in the near-blackness in front of him.

It knows about guns, he thought, feeling a warm trickle down his right side. The korrigan might have no idea what a gun was, but it knew humans were dangerous holding metal—and almost helpless without it.

The korrigan was stalking, getting perfect position.

Greg scrambled backwards. He tripped over something and fell again, his left hand landing in a big pile of debris, earth, and rags.

And eggs.

Something like a chicken egg, twice as big, more symmetrical, his fingers told him. The shell seemed a little leathery. Sporkin's comment on sexes and breeding flashed through his mind. This was the safe place, and the thing in here with him was the female.

Greg picked up an egg and threw it hard at the spot where he guessed the korrigan was. It hit with a wet smashing noise, and there was the first sound he'd ever heard a korrigan make—a weird, high-pitched creak that resembled nothing Greg had ever heard but whose meaning was unmistakable. He threw another egg and then rolled toward where he thought the gun was as the korrigan hurtled through space and landed where he'd just been.

Guard your nest, dammit, Greg screamed silently.

He found the barrel, hefted the gun, and turned and shot blindly four times. The flashes framed the korrigan bent over its nest. It turned and leaped at him. Greg fired again, thought he hit it, felt claws like scalpels slice open his left cheek. He fired again, and the thing was scrabbling away from him as the echoes boomed in the enclosed space.

Greg felt for the matches, his head swimming.

By the sound, the thing was at the nest again.

Greg found the matches, lit one, and threw it into the nearby shelving. He threw another, and something caught.

There was an old dresser beside him. Flames from the shelves licked up its side, gobbling the ancient wood and varnish.

With a heave, Greg brought the dresser crashing down between himself and the korrigan. One whole side of the basement was lit now by burning wood, and the creature hunched where it was, apparently torn between the need to escape, the need to protect, and the need to kill.

Greg shoved an old chest under the window, his right arm and left ankle screaming in pain. He climbed up, desperately fast, picturing a last leap from the furious korrigan. He hauled himself up and out, panting. He rolled over and scrambled away, holding his gun on the window.

Flames licked around the opening. Greg's shoulder and whole right side hurt like hell. Where were the cops?

A SWAT team came pouring down the alley.

Hands grabbed him and pulled him further from the house. Greg heard someone shout for a paramedic and wondered vaguely who the injured person might be. Through the fog of pain, he could tell one hand was softer and warmer than the others. He dropped his gun and clung to that hand as blood and hurt, and fire swirled through his head.

* * *

White.

Somebody in white, and a white room.

A face swam into view, slowly becoming clearer. Below it was a white uniform and a name tag that said Rolli.

The nurse turned. "I think he's coming out of it."

"Out of what?" Greg asked, tongue thick in his dry mouth.

"Out of the Nembutal," the nurse said. "You've had a good day's sleep."

"Day?"

"It's Friday evening."

Friday, Greg thought. He'd been in L.A. since—what? The preceding Tuesday? That sounded right. He tried to remember the sequence of events that got him here.

Then the nurse was gone, and Julie was there.

"Hi, hero."

Greg remembered the preceding night. "No hero." He realized the side of his face and his right shoulder were bandaged. There was a sling of some kind holding his right arm still, and something tight was wrapped around his ribs. His ankle throbbed a little, too. "Just an idiot."

"Sporkin may think so," she said, pulling over a chair and sinking into it. "You killed his last possible specimen."

"I killed more than that," Greg said. He saw a water pitcher on the bedside table and motioned toward it. Julie poured him a glass, and he drank quickly.

"There were eggs down there, in a nest. The others ducked into the gym for a reason—to lead everyone away from the female while she got back to the nest. It would have worked if she hadn't picked the wrong time to pop out in front of us.

"By the way, I burned the place down on purpose. I didn't have to, I guess. It just seemed like an inspiration."

"It sounds like a damn good idea to me. It's really over now."

"Are they sure?"

She nodded. "Half the LAPD has been through that area. They're still looking, but they're pretty sure that's it."

"It in this country, maybe. In England, who knows? There could be a hundred or a thousand still dormant, buried under dolmens."

"They'll find them, Greg. Everyone knows about them now, thanks to you."

"And you—and a lot of good people." He thought about Welles and Fernandez.

"By the way, they finally found that truck. The one that hit Captain Lear."

"And?"

"It would have been a dead end," she said. "The driver was stoned. He doesn't remember any of it."

"Another item for Welles' ten-percent file. The stuff that never fits or never gets solved. Did they ever find Martin's aide, that guy McGraw?"

"Yes. Or at least, they found his body hidden in a sewer."

Both fell silent, looking at each other's faces. Greg knew she was wondering, as he was, who would bring up what they both knew was the next topic.

He steeled himself emotionally. "I guess we need to talk about us some time."

"Remember those old movies we used to watch? The Bogie and Bacall ones?"

"Yes," Greg said with a thin smile.

"I suppose in one of those, this is where you'd say, 'Doll, I know now what's been missing from my life—you.' And I'd say something like, 'You know, maybe out there is a sunset we should be riding off into.'"

"I doubt Bacall ever said that in a movie, but she should have," he said.

Julie looked down for a moment, then back into his eyes. "I do think we have to talk, but I don't know what I'm trying to say. In some ways, I haven't said goodbye to Walt yet."

"I think I understand. A psychologist would say the trauma interrupted the normal grieving process. Take all the time you need for that. In the meantime, I'm here if you need to talk—or whatever."

"And I'm here when you need to talk," she said. "Maybe that idea of a vacation wasn't too far off," she said. "But not Alaska. I hate the cold."

"Then let's head for the Bahamas."

"I feel like I have to say it again. No promises. I'm still numb in a lot of ways, and I don't know how I'll feel about you or me or anything else after that wears off. We'll just have to take our chances."

"We're friends, Julie. We're going off on a break as friends. No pressure. Besides, I'm still trying to sort out myself, too. I haven't forgotten what I said about being disengaged. Maybe I can fund a good cause off the rights to my take on it and actually show up and do something."

"I said you were a good man. I have some ideas percolating, too."

Greg thought a moment. "We didn't have a choice in anything we did, I guess, but I can understand Sporkin's thinking. Doesn't say much for the human race, does it? We meet another intelligent species, and we immediately wipe it out. Damn it, I wish somehow we hadn't had to do that. Science must be going crazy."

"I never thought of scientists as a mob, but they are now. And I get a ton of messages from the cryptozoologists. They think we validated their whole field."

"Well, we did more than validate it. We expanded it. Cryptozoologists used to think things like the yeti, if they existed, were survivors or offshoots of lineages we knew about. Now we've proven there can be survivors from lineages we never knew existed."

"Sporkin's the center of all that. I hear he already has an agent and a lawyer. Oh, and guess what, lawyer? Tom Cooley got ahold of him using my name and made a deal to represent him. He didn't even tell me he was doing it. I never thought he was that much of an asshole. Anyway, Sporkin's going to be the most famous scientist since Einstein."

"Did you quit the firm?"

Her lips tightened. "Couldn't. I made a deal. Tom gave me the firm's help on things like restraining orders and media while I'm living in a hotel under a fake name. My sister got here, and she's been driving me around in a rental while I wear a wig and sunglasses."

"I can get my publisher to help a lot if I promise them the first chance to buy my book rights from this. Handle sales of media rights, that sort of thing. Help make sure we get a chance to tell the true story because I'll bet it's already being lost. From what you said, I take it the three-ring media circus has already started."

"That's an understatement. The six biggest networks all sent their damn anchors here."

"I'd hate to be Henderson or Creighton. The media and the scientific world are going to second-guess the hell out of them for doing their jobs and eliminating a threat to citizens instead of going all out for a live specimen."

"Henderson's been elbowed out of the picture. Mayor Neilson and Chief Aldridge, who, by the way, would like to be Mayor himself in two years, are making all the announcements now that the case is solved. We're elbowed out, too. The city wants to downplay how they only handled this because two civilians told them what to do."

"Jerks."

"Jerks or not, it helps. The media would be even worse if they weren't downgrading us to 'helpful witnesses' in the briefings.

"I did one interview with KTSG because of Karen Montrose but kept it short. That was just before the FBI, of all people, asked me to pause interviews, which I was totally grateful for. I still want to get out of here for a while. And I want it to be with you because you're the only one I can talk to who knows what it was like. After that— well, we'll see."

"I'll take my chances."

29

This is all. This is all of the Clan.

The dying screams of the others still echoing, even though they had been far apart when death came.

We are all that is left.

A Clan of only two. Two running through the Stinking Holes until the Holes ended. Then, over hills and through trees, into a land where no trees grew and Tall Ones were scattered. Exhausted. But safe, safe for now.

Only two. But one was a Life Bringer.

The Clan must survive.

ACKNOWLEDGMENTS

The creation of this novel and this new edition was a long journey. I thank the public relations staff of the Los Angeles Police Department for assisting with the research on this novel. I also appreciate the support of my friends at Hangar 1 and that of my agent, Connor Smith of Hesperides Literary.

I thank everyone who read this manuscript and provided comments, including my wonderful writing mentor, the late and much missed Ann Crispin, the font of advice and wisdom known as Steve Saffel, biologist Susan Hazlett, Carol and Tim Hightshoe, Chris Broyhill (who doubled as my weapons consultant), Terrie Wolf, Kris Winkler, Amber Fraley, Chad Arment, and others. Thanks to all those who have encouraged my writing, including, of course, my mother, Jane Bille, my late father, Don Bille, my wife Deb, my brother Joel, my sisters Aileen and Sarah, my daughters Lauryn and Corey, and friends like Gregg Anderson, Robyn Kane, Barry and Kirsty Smith, and Liz Ruth. Fellow authors who lent support or encouragement over the long gestation period of this novel included LJ Hachmeister (God rest you, my friend), Jonathan Maberry, Anne Larsen, Chris Mandeville, J. T. Evans, Tonya Atkinson, Melissia Marie Rolli, Meghan O'Neill Muriel, John Patterson, Paul Kolodziejski, Barbara Buffington, and many more. Then there is the rest of the tribe at Superstars and the Pikes Peak Writers Club, the most supportive groups any writer could ask for. I appreciate you, one and all.

ABOUT THE AUTHOR

Matt Bille is an author in Colorado Springs, Colorado. He is also a naturalist, historian, science writer, and defense consultant. A former Air Force officer, he is the lead author of the NASA-published history *The First Space Race: Launching the World's First Satellites* (2004), a groundbreaking account of the early Space Age. He has written three books on the world's rarest and least-known animals, *Rumors of Existence* (1995, *Shadows of Existence* (2006), and *Of Book sand Beasts: A Cryptozoologist's Library* (2021). He is a member of the National Association of Science Writers and the History Committee of the American Institute of Aeronautics and Astronautics.

He appeared on two television programs on mystery animals and blogs on the latest science and technology news at *Matt's Sci/Tech Blog*, http://mattbille.blogspot.com.

For news on his current and future books, visit Matt's website at www.mattbilleauthor.com or contact him at mattsciwriter@proton mail.com.

ALSO BY MATT BILLE

Of Books and Beasts: A Cryptozoologist's Library

AFTERWORD

Go to hangaripublishing.com to learn more about the Authors and stay up to date with their newest releases.

www.ingramcontent.com/pod-product-compliance
Lightning Source LLC
Chambersburg PA
CBHW061727120626
46550CB00005B/1729